ALAN JAMES was born in 1940. At the age of 28, he ordained as a Buddhist monk in London; after the death of his teacher, Kapilavaddho Bhikkhu, he completed his training in Thailand. In 1980 he co-founded the House of Inner Tranquillity, a meditation centre in Bradford on Avon.

As a result of the growth of the meditation centre and the increasing number of students who wished to train full-time, Alan established two monasteries (for monks and nuns respectively). The course of monastic training is firmly based in the model laid down by the Buddha in the Pali Canon, but adapted to a modern western cultural setting.

Today, Alan continues to teach the path to enlightenment, as well as directing the development of the monasteries and meditation centre. There are also groups under his instruction in London, Oxford and Toronto.

Alan lives in Wiltshire with his wife Christine.

THE UNFOLDING
OF WISDOM

THE UNFOLDING
OF WISDOM

The Buddha's Path to Enlightenment

ALAN JAMES

AUKANA
Bradford on Avon

Reprinted 1998

Aukana Trust,
9 Masons Lane, Bradford on Avon BA15 1QN, England

The Aukana Trust is a registered charity (No 326938)

Typeset in Palatino 11/12.5 by LP&TS Ltd, Somerton
Printed in Great Britain by Redwood Books, Trowbridge

Cover photograph copyright © Andrew Brock 1993
Cover printed by Devenish & Co, Bath

British Library Cataloguing in Publication Data

James, Alan
   Unfolding of Wisdom: Buddha's Path to
   Enlightenment
   I. Title
   294.3

   ISBN 0-9511769-4-3 (hardback)
   ISBN 0-9511769-5-1 (softback)

ACKNOWLEDGEMENTS

The publishers would like to thank **Andrew Brock** for
kindly allowing us to use the cover photograph,
and the **Pali Text Society** for permission to quote
from their copyright translations of the Pali Canon.

CONTENTS

INTRODUCTION

The Teaching of the Buddha is an impeccable and systematic way to truth that offers safe passage across the deserts of despair and anguish. I hope that this collection of talks will open a door for those who, pondering on the mysteries of life, are looking for a way to find further answers.

This book is a selection of lectures given mainly in the last five years and chosen to reflect different levels of interest in the subject. Inevitably, important aspects of this complex and extensive Teaching are not represented, while others are dealt with several times. I have tried to organise the material in a way that minimises these shortcomings and would like especially to thank Robert Mann and Rose Youd for their considered and helpful advice.

I am persuaded that some personal details are necessary as an introduction to the author and to give this collection of talks a background. What follows does not seem to me particularly worthy of recording, for I only did what I was driven to do, often in spite of myself – and much of that was painful at the time. Truth has a way of calling to its devotees that brooks no argument, no matter how much one may protest the summons.

My own quest goes back almost as far as I can remember. A love of the natural world meant much time spent alone, often wondering about the place of human beings in the scheme of things. Unable to 'have faith' as a local priest advised, question followed question. What was life all about? Was telepathy real? Was it possible to be conscious outside one's physical body and to visit far-off places? Why were we here? What was the purpose of it all?

Trying to enlist cooperation for experiments with astral travel and communication in dreams, I drove friends to invent fictitious psychic events to keep me quiet. Occasional experiences of the paranormal pushed me onwards, though, and provided tantalising hints of levels of existence beyond the one we all know. I opted to study physics at university, believing naively that it could uncover the secrets of the cosmos. Discovering its limitations, downcast, I lost enthusiasm for the endless cramming necessary to pass exams. Instead, my attention turned to Indian philosophy and Oriental religious beliefs.

With such a disparity of interests, it is perhaps no wonder that I chose to 'drop out'. After an intervening year of work to accumulate funds I boarded ship for India, home of spirituality for thousands of years. I was then 22. Determined to find the Answer, I bought only a one-way ticket and took all the money I had, the grand sum of £100.

I found that travelling alone is a great privilege, for people welcome the single person into their lives with a warmth and honesty they deny couples or groups. Staying in ashrams, visiting gurus and holy men, talking with 'ordinary' people, I met men and women wise in the ways of the world and in the intricacies of mind and spirit. They taught me invaluable lessons, sometimes without meaning to, sometimes with a directness that shocked.

This visit was to produce little more than a realisation that running away from the Western world was no solution to the problem; if an answer was to be found it had to be found there. So, against the advice of officialdom, I made my way back to England through Pakistan, Afghanistan, Persia (as it was then), Turkey and finally Europe. Everywhere I met with amazing kindness and hospitality, and to this day feel privileged to have met so many 'foreign' people all of whom were warm and friendly human beings, whatever their circumstances.

If running away from the Western world was no solution, then it seemed reasonable to embrace it more enthusiastically than I had to date. After recuperating and working for a while I emigrated to Canada where, I felt sure, I could better enjoy the advantages the West has to offer. It was an interesting time and served to underline the fact that there is more to life than material wealth and well-being.

A second trip to India produced little more than the first. The quest for truth seemed irresolvable. This was a miserable few months, for nothing seemed to work and there seemed no answer to be found anywhere. Back in England, despairing, a headline in a Sunday paper caught my eye: 'Barman becomes Buddhist Monk,' it shouted. If Buddhism will accept a barman, I thought, then perhaps there is hope yet. It was one of the few paths I had not examined in detail.

After enquiries, I contacted the 'barman', now the Venerable Kapilavaddho Bhikkhu, a Theravada Buddhist monk ordained in the Thai tradition. He became my spiritual mentor and I joined as a probationer the monastic community of which he was abbot. About ten years previously and then a lay man, he had served behind a bar part-time for a few weeks as a favour for a friend. So much for newspaper headlines. But this one saved my life.

Always a loner, and with a dread of being labelled as a member of a group or organisation, I had fought shy of signing up for anything. Now, I could see no way to get what I wanted – understanding – without sacrificing my independence in the worst way imaginable. I became a Buddhist monk with shaved head and eyebrows and wearing nothing but a couple of cotton robes, one of them a skirt. In India it might not have been so bad, but in London ... The anticipation was worse than the event, as always, and so began the most demanding, exciting and rewarding period in my life. The Buddha's Teaching, challenging yet precise and provable, conveyed by a man who would stand no nonsense from anyone, was everything I had been looking for.

☆ ☆ ☆

With hindsight it is obvious that I had no choice but to pursue my quest, wherever it led. Though uncomfortable and often unpopular, following my own intuitions and concerns felt right, as though I were doing what had to be done. True to a childhood maxim, it did 'come out all right in the end' – though the preparations seemed endless.

It all looks quite different now. It seems so obvious that I sometimes wonder why others cannot see it, and forget that it took me nearly twenty years to find the answer. Looking back, I remember finding the whole matter just as obscure and frustrating as students do today.

I have often wondered how best I could convey the things I learned over many years of often painful enquiry. Having passed the age of 50 – and been teaching one thing and another for a long time now – I have found that there are some things you can teach easily and some you cannot. It's those you cannot that have taxed me greatly.

How do you teach someone to learn from experience? How do you teach someone to pay minute attention to every action, to every thought, to every intention? How do you teach someone the joy of discovery? How do you teach someone that a habitual mode of behaviour is harmful? How do you teach someone to change the way he or she learns? Sometimes, perhaps even most times, you just cannot. People can and will go only at their own pace and in their own direction.

Why teach at all? And yet, however inept one might be, it is better than not teaching. Perhaps it is truer to say that it is not so much teaching as collaborating, working together with a student to find the best solution to an individual problem. I know that my own journey was possible only because of the opportunity to meet and talk with those more experienced in the quest for truth. I owe an inexpressible debt of gratitude to all those people, some remembered, some forgotten, some indelibly imprinted in mind. Attempting to help others when they ask in their turn seems the least I can do.

No searching for truth is ever wasted. If it seems that there are no answers to be found, it may be that you have not yet learned to look and listen in the right way. I have no hesitation in recommending the Teaching of the Buddha as one of the supreme ways to overcome the perils of the world and to find the answers that the few have always sought.

Alan James
House of Inner Tranquillity
May 1993

1

THE COMPLETE PATH

Enlightenment, the cessation of suffering, is like the top of a mountain: no matter which path you choose to climb to it, the summit remains the same. But the paths to the summit vary greatly. What you learn on your journey will depend upon the route you take.

Every path is different. All cultures, in all ages, have had their enlightened individuals and their paths to truth and freedom. North America, Africa, Australia, India, the Middle East, Europe – all of them had and still have their wise men. These men created all the paths there ever were, drawing on their own experience, culture and conditioning.

The goal is the same but the paths vary dramatically. Even within Buddha Dhamma, the Teaching of the Buddha, there are different paths. The Buddha himself originally taught two quite different approaches to the quest for freedom from suffering. He taught the meditative path of tranquillity and calming on the one hand, and the path of 'dry' insight on the other. True, he conjoined them, but even today they exist as two distinct approaches to the one goal. From its origins in the valley and flood plains of the River Ganges in India, Buddhism has spread across the world. In the two and a half millennia of its existence, many more paths have developed.

Look at just some of the ways in which the established kinds of Buddhism differ: Theravada places its accent on the original Teaching; Tibetan Buddhism has developed a range of gods and demons, bodhisattvas and reincarnated teachers; Japanese Zen appears to reject the books and study in favour of its love of *koan* and shock tactics. Because so different, each path cultivates and develops distinctive strengths and attitudes in its followers. The same is true of other established ways to liberation.

Consider for a moment two of the paths of yoga, the Hindu

system. *Hatha-yoga* (sometimes called physical yoga) develops an intimate knowledge of the body and its workings, and awesome skills of bodily control. *Bhakti-yoga* on the other hand, the yoga of devotion, develops something quite different. It is not particularly concerned with the physical as such but practises and develops all the pathways and byways of love and devotion.

Occultism, both East and West, develops yet other qualities and strengths – things like psychic powers, with stress on and training in the use of will-power to get desired results. Australian Aboriginal paths develop telepathy and mental control, among other things.

And what of Buddhism? Buddha Dhamma in all its various manifestations has a complete range of effective paths for the seeker. Looking at the better-known aspects of Buddhism, we can readily identify some major differences between them. In Theravada there is a great stress on personal endeavour, precision and the traditional teachings. Tibetan Buddhism has a great love of ceremony and magic, art and cosmology. Zen favours simplicity, asceticism and paradox. Each of these paths develops different characteristics in its followers. Whatever positive characteristic you want or need to develop, whether devotion or intellect, mental power or patience, compassion or wisdom, Buddhism has the answer.

Whatever path you choose, the efforts to master it are similar. All paths without exception need dedication and commitment; they need a great deal of work. Seeking the end of anguish is not an easy task, even though it is towards that end that we all direct our efforts. All of us seek to avoid or to eliminate suffering, whether it is something as simple as taking an aspirin for a headache or as complex as trying to realise enlightenment. All of us seek to avoid pain and suffering.

Repeatedly making mistaken choices of method, most of us gradually learn what is effective and what is not. We might try things like working all the time to avoid contemplation of our difficulties. Some of us take to drink, some to drugs; some try promiscuity or constant entertainment. Gambling is another attempted escape: if only we could make that big win, then all our troubles would be over. Of course it does not quite work like that. I remember hearing of a selection of twenty Football Pools winners who had won very large sums, and only one of whom was both alive and still happy. He was a clergyman who had given away most of his winnings.

Man has tried everything to alleviate suffering, often as not increasing it considerably. However ill-advised the method, the motivation is always to reduce or eliminate personal anguish and distress.

On any path you have to strive with great diligence, trying to hold in mind that the goal is attainable in this life, here and now. 'Strive with diligence' were the Buddha's last words and, for some, have caused no end of trouble.

One man read that to get the best out of meditation you need to choose the posture most suited to your particular mental and physical type. He read, further, that to find which of the four postures (standing, sitting, lying down or walking) suited you best, you should try each for three days. So he spent 72 hours, non-stop, meditating in the sitting posture. Once he had got the kinks out of his legs and recovered from the ordeal, he tried to walk non-stop for 72 hours. He did not properly understand the import of what he had read.

To strive with diligence means that you should do your normal quota of meditation, and try those hours in one posture for three normal days. For a meditating monk, this might be anything from five to ten separate hours a day in his normal schedule – **separate** hours. The advice is very sensible: you will soon get to know whether one posture suits you better than the others.

The interpretation of 'strive with diligence' is full of traps for the unwary, especially in the West where we tend to work with great enthusiasm but little patience.

☆ ☆ ☆

How do you choose one path out of the many? They offer such a plethora of different attributes, attitudes, approaches and skills. What factors influence the best choice of path for any single individual? There are quite a few.

Upbringing in this life is a significant one. Whether you have been born West or East makes an enormous difference to what might suit you. In the West we are strongly individualistic and often challenge at every turn those with authority and experience. That is in complete contrast to the East, where teachers are revered and their instructions followed without question.

If you have a strong Western conditioning, you – with Frank Sinatra – will want to say 'I did it my way', and may not take easily to a teacher telling you what to do. Some Westerners find it improbable that anyone can be more expert than they in anything at all, but this extreme attitude is usually moderated for most seekers by other conditions. One of those is past-life conditioning.

Some who come here, although Westerners born and raised, feel very much at home with an Oriental teaching. It leads one to suppose that perhaps they are reborn Orientals. Those of you who have read *Life as a Siamese Monk* by the Venerable Kapilavaddho Bhikkhu will know that he describes many lives in an Oriental setting before one or two in the West. Once, when talking about his past, he said that it was as though in a life of a hundred years he had spent ninety-eight of those years in the East and only two in the West. He had spent countless lifetimes born in the East, absorbing all its culture and conditioning, and only a few in the Western world. No wonder he felt at home with an Oriental teaching. I think perhaps others of us here may have a similar history.

Others of course find Buddha Dhamma quite unfamiliar, to the point of being very difficult to understand. It is tempting to suppose that these people have been born as Westerners again and again, and have had little contact with an Oriental way of any description. Their difficulty in understanding is readily apparent, usually at the initial interview. We may suggest that such a seeker would be more likely to feel at home in Roman Catholicism, which has been in the West for about fifteen hundred years, or in Western Occultism, which has been around much longer.

The Western accent on self may also be moderated by another form of conditioning, which I have called philosophical awareness for want of a better term. Quite a few people have sought their spiritual fortune in far-flung corners of the world. In the process they have acquired a good understanding of the demands of the spiritual search. Their own search may have taken them to places like India, Sri Lanka, Thailand and places even further east. Having absorbed some of the necessities of the way from such experiences, they feel much more in tune with a teaching like Buddhism. Other people may not have travelled in the physical sense but may, instead, have read extensively. That too can be a tremendous benefit.

You also need personal dedication. How far are you prepared to go? What sacrifices are you prepared to make? Would you give up everything to follow the spiritual path? Or do you want to hang on to a few necessities, just in case? Let us look at the options.

☆ ☆ ☆

Firstly, where should you seek to train in the way to enlightenment? Where is the best place in the world to follow the spiritual path? Is it the mystic East, supposedly the home of such things from ancient times? Or can one do it in the West?

To read about the East, to see films and pictures, does not easily convey what it is like to live there. In general, the Westerner finds it difficult to adapt, although many do succeed eventually. Here are some examples of the problems we can face when seeking our spiritual fortunes in the East. In each case I have illustrated the worst that can happen. While some may not experience such extreme difficulty, it is never an easy matter to adapt to an alien climate and culture.

For those of us born in northern temperate climes, the climate over most of the East is awful. It is debilitating and takes years to adjust to, if you can. It is really very hard work. Even the residents of those lands have difficulty. The Westerner pitchforked into it can find it tough, to say the least.

What about custom, culture? To state the obvious, it is foreign. It takes years to learn so as never to offend, and includes all kinds of things to which we in the West are most likely unaccustomed: things like sitting cross-legged. Most of us can manage to sit in this way for short periods of time, often with our knees up round our ears. Conditioned to sitting in chairs, we usually experience great discomfort after half an hour or so. A monk might sit in no other way, day after day, for many hours each day.

The Venerable Kapilavaddho had severe arthritis, and when he went to Thailand to ordain as a monk at the age of forty-seven, he (like everybody else) had to sit cross-legged. With arthritis in the hips, knees and ankles, it was really very difficult. He showed me a photograph of the contraption he had devised to try to force his legs into the required position.

He had a wooden bed to each side of which he had screwed a

large metal hook. Around the hooks he would wind lengths of rope, which he would then pass round his knees. Pulling hard on the ropes forced his knees down towards the bed, and in this way he hoped to get into an approximation of the posture required by custom. Never one to give in to anything, he came painfully close to the required posture, but was never comfortable, as you can imagine.

What about the food out East? It is possible to find sustaining food but generally it is poor, it is unpalatable and quite often not sufficiently nutritious even for those used to it. When I first arrived in India, although feeling very much at home, I found the food impossible and was unable to eat anything for ten days. Realising I could just waste away, I managed to force myself to eat, but never really got used to the diet. They say that if you stay long enough – about five years – you can get acclimatised to the food. It's a long time, isn't it?

The language is incomprehensible without major efforts, for it is not based on those we are familiar with, like French, German and Latin. There are different alphabets and different sounds. In India, I worked hard to learn some very basic Hindustani. To my dismay, the teacher I finally chose to study with did not speak Hindi at all. He spoke Gujerati, the language of his own locality (only about seventy or eighty miles away from where I had originally been based). Gujerati is totally different from Hindi: it has different spoken and written alphabets and is a completely different language. I felt so disheartened that I was disinclined to follow my teacher's request that I learn his language.

Further east, the problems multiply. Languages like Thai and Chinese are based on tonal systems, where the same sound pitched high or low means different things – an added complication for Westerners. In the East there are huge communication difficulties, even when English can be used as a common language. The 'mind-set' is so different that communication is very often at cross-purposes.

What about teachers? The East is the home of the spiritual search, we believe, so surely there must be lots of teachers. Well of course there are, and there are a few very good ones. Depending where you go, however, there may be none at all. When visiting various monasteries and meditation centres in Thailand I found that in some places there was no teacher available at all.

To my surprise, it turned out that quite a few people in the 'mystic East' really did not know an awful lot. Both local people and Westerners, living in the country to follow the spiritual path, often had some very strange notions about Buddhism.

I met some Western monks at a monastery and meditation centre in Bangkok. In conversation with them it transpired that some of them had not even heard of the four noble truths[1]. Admittedly they had been ordained only a matter of weeks, but it seemed to me almost inconceivable that an ordained monk could be so ignorant of the Teaching. Some of these men were struggling with a system rendered incomprehensible by the total absence of guidance. There was no real training at all. They were expected to sort it out for themselves. They really did not know what to do for the best.

Some Eastern monks are not much better off. Although they do usually receive instruction in the training, it is often of poor quality. At one place I visited, two of the Oriental monks had committed suicide the previous year because they had been over-zealous in their practice. They had gone wrong and there was no one there to correct them. There are considerable problems in finding the right teacher in the East.

Where there is training, there are many different approaches to it. Not all the teachers teach the right thing. As an added complication, some Oriental teachers do not believe that a Westerner could ever be capable of learning about the spiritual path. Standards vary enormously.

So how do you find out which path is for you? What happens if you get caught up in something like the Rajneesh sex scandal? He took the view that the way to overcome a problem is to practise it extensively until you get bored with it. However attractive that might seem, it does not work that way.

On the other hand, the support of teachers and seekers, meditators, in the East is very good, even outstanding, in all respects. *Dāna* – giving, generosity – is well-practised and thoroughly understood, and that is a major difference in attitude

---

[1] Four noble truths: four statements made by the Buddha to summarise his entire Teaching. They are: (i) there is suffering (*dukkha*); (ii) there is a cause of suffering; (iii) there is the complete cessation of suffering; (iv) there is a path leading to the cessation of suffering. Truths (i) and (ii) identify the problem (anguish) and its cause (craving based on ignorance). Truths (iii) and (iv) identify the goal (*nibbāna*) and the method of realising it (the eightfold path).

from the West.

What about Buddhism in the West? How might the spiritual seeker fare?

Climate, custom, food and language are all generally all right. There are some minor variations from region to region and country to country, but scarcely any trauma. Occasionally you find an import of Oriental custom, such as chanting or sitting cross-legged, but it is quite possible to avoid those if you feel the need.

What about teachers? Teachers are of differing standards, naturally enough. Most take as a guideline the traditional works of the branch of Buddhism they profess; occasionally they are more book-knowledgeable than their Oriental counterparts. Some suffer from a lack of experiential understanding. Some suggest that *sīla*, ethical discipline, is not necessary, and others that *sīla* is the whole path, instead of a necessary preparation.

Support can be a serious problem in the West, because *dāna*, generosity, is often not understood. If you look at the history of monastic institutions in the West, you find that they have had to support themselves by something like farming or tourism.

I once visited an abbey on the edge of Dartmoor. I found that they have quite a thriving business. There is a large shop that sells pottery made by the monks, wooden bowls that the monks have turned and all kinds of souvenirs and knick-knacks. Much of their support comes from the sale of such things to the tourists who visit the abbey. The fact that such an enterprise is necessary illustrates the relative scarcity of free generosity in the West. It also shows how fortunate we are here, at the House of Inner Tranquillity, that people are so keen to support the place both financially and with their time and effort. It allows things here to work very smoothly without having to resort to trading.

So where should you choose to train, East or West?

One of my lasting impressions of the East is the great number of seemingly conflicting approaches to the spiritual path. It is a wonder that anyone gets anywhere. Many paths seemed utterly bizarre and insisted on customs and practices that have no relevance whatever to the spiritual search: one sect' in India worshipped **rats**, for instance. You could spend a lifetime researching all the options and never have time for any real work.

On balance, I think the West is the better place to train, whether or not you can find a teacher with experiential knowledge. Obviously if you can find a teacher with experiential knowledge then there is no need to look any further. If you cannot, it is still best to do your study here and then go East, if you feel you must. The reason is this. Having trained in the West and then decided to travel to the East, you will be able to sort out the wheat from the chaff much more easily. Armed with at least an intellectual understanding of the Teaching, you will be in a better position to assess any meditation centre or teacher you visit. There is one danger, however. You may fall into the trap – as do so many Westerners – of believing that you know it all.

☆ ☆ ☆

Having decided where, now we turn to what. What kind of path suits you best? There are two major types. I have called them the direct path and the complete path.

Direct paths aim one-pointedly at enlightenment in the shortest possible time. They cut out everything that is not immediately relevant to that single task, believing all else to be a distraction. These paths are often called short or fast. Those who walk on direct paths tend towards the view that only my way is right, and sometimes appear to lack humanity. They can appear selfish to outsiders.

Fast paths develop only supramundane[2] wisdom, the wisdom that recognises all things to be unsatisfactory, transient and non-self. They undoubtedly lead to enlightenment, but at a cost: they do not develop mundane[3] skills, mundane knowledge, mundane wisdom.

Complete paths, on the other hand, are paths that emphasise the importance to the human race of a more rounded training.

---

[2] Supramundane: above or beyond (supra) worldly (mundane) existence, considered as the sphere in which ignorance (of the truth of things as they are) operates. Supramundane wisdom is wisdom leading to enlightenment, the cessation of ignorance and therefore of craving and the suffering (*dukkha*) it produces.

[3] Mundane: of the world(s). The mundane worlds comprise 31 levels of existence divided into three. First is the world of sensuous craving (*kāma-loka*) including hell states, the animal realm, the human realm and a number of terrestrial heavens. Next is the world of refined matter (*rūpa-loka*), various levels of existence where sensuous craving is absent. Lastly comes the 'formless' world (*arūpa-loka*), where all trace of materiality is transcended. Each of these worlds is still relative and conditioned and beings in them are still in thrall to ignorance. Mundane wisdom is that which allows the happiest and most successful functioning at any of these levels.

These paths nurture and develop the finer feelings, the human graces and efforts made on behalf of others rather than just for oneself. They are slower and surer than the direct variety but have added rewards for the seeker. Complete paths tend towards nurturing; they tend towards compassion. From the outside, people see them as unselfish.

In addition to supramundane wisdom, complete paths take care to develop mundane wisdom. Mundane wisdom shows how the world works. It breeds tolerance and compassion for all things and all beings. It is the wisdom that allows harmony and peace to operate between all beings.

The Buddha was often asked if all enlightened people were the same. He said that in one way they were the same – and in another way they were not. All enlightenment is the same enlightenment. The top of the mountain is not different for some. People taking both fast and slow paths arrive at the same place. But all paths are not the same, even within Buddhism.

The Buddha said that on balance he preferred the company of those who had taken the slower, more roundabout path to enlightenment. He indicated that they were easier to live with, more rounded, more competent, more satisfying company than those who had travelled the fast path alone. He strongly advised the many recluses who had become enlightened on the fast path to develop concentration for 'ease of living here and now'. Though they were enlightened, he recommended that they continued training in slow-path methods to develop the mundane skills essential for good relations with others and for proficiency in the day-to-day world.

☆ ☆ ☆

So what are the major differences between fast and slow paths, between direct and complete paths? In the short time we have available this evening, I can probably illustrate them best by describing a caricature of a typical traveller on each path. Though a caricature inevitably distorts some features, a comprehensive overview of the differences would need an entire series of talks.

The fast-path traveller develops only as much concentration as he needs to practise *vipassanā*[4], thus to gain supramundane

---

[4]   *Vipassanā*: insight meditation. Essentially development of awareness of the transient nature of all relative things and experiences.

insight. His only interest is in suppressing the hindrances enough to pay attention to transience, unsatisfactoriness and non-self (*anicca*, *dukkha* and *anattā*). He may not bother overmuch with keeping the precepts[5] or with study, for he does not really see the point of practising anything other than *vipassanā*, the quicker to become enlightened. In this regard, the fast-path traveller may see loving-kindness meditation[6] as a waste of time. If he does spend any time on it, he feels anxious and as though he is playing games when he should be working; he should be working at 'the real thing', *vipassanā*, to reach the end of the path in the shortest possible time.

The fast-path traveller may be an iconoclast. He may tear down others' belief systems and be intolerant of other approaches to the spiritual search. Narrow in outlook, blinkered, he may be unaware of the feelings and problems of others, even those to whom he is physically close. He knows little – and sometimes cares less – about the workings of the world in relative terms. Often very efficient in a mechanical way, he upsets others because he does not consider their feelings. The fast-path traveller tends towards impatience, believes in the adage 'every man for himself' and seldom thinks of giving anything back to the world. You could say he is low on gratitude. He will probably get enlightened more quickly than someone on the slow path, however.

What about the slow-path traveller? The slow-path traveller develops tranquillity, concentration and mundane wisdom as well as *vipassanā* leading to supramundane insight. He not only keeps the precepts, although without being too rigid about it, but also is strong in loving-kindness and compassion. Devoting at least as much time to loving-kindness meditation as to *vipassanā*, he may also develop the jhanas (the fixed meditations)[7], as well as some or all of the psychic powers.

---

5   Precepts: rules of training. For the lay individual these number five: to refrain from (i) killing or harming living beings; (ii) taking that which is not given; (iii) unlawful sexual practices; (iv) lying and harsh speech; (v) strong drink or psychotropic drugs. Keeping the precepts calms the mind, rendering it fit for meditation by the elimination of guilt and shame.

6   Loving-kindness (*mettā*): a meditation designed to develop a mind full of love and friendliness towards all beings. It counteracts hatred and has many benefits. See Chapter 11 for a fuller explanation.

7   Fixed meditation (*jhāna*): fully conscious meditation withdrawn from the physical senses. It is 'fixed' because it is unshakeable by the mental hindrances.

The psychic powers are various. You can project yourself as one individual or as many individuals on the psychic levels; you can walk through walls, fly through the air, swim in the earth and travel to the moon. The vehicle you use is not the physical body, of course, but the mental body; the powers are a development of mind.

Another psychic power is the divine ear. This allows the meditator to hear sounds that are normally inaccessible, such as those at a distance, and thus to know what is going on in remote places. Another is to know the minds of others, to be aware of what people are thinking and of their states of mind.

The slow-path traveller may develop the divine eye. This would allow him to see things normally invisible because of size or distance or because they belong to other levels of existence. With this power, he can see the birth and death of beings. He can see someone die in this life and be born again in another place, another condition, another level, another life. Developing the divine eye might also, with additional training, lead to knowledge of his own and others' past lives.

Another power, this time common to both direct and complete paths, is the extinction of cankers[8], the path that leads to enlightenment itself. Mastering this psychic power develops the ability to see transience, unsatisfactoriness and non-self so that all ignorance, craving and hatred are eradicated.

The slow-path traveller, the complete-path traveller, may develop some or all of the psychic powers. Whether he does or not, he necessarily will have a much greater feel for the world, for other people and for relationships between beings. You can see that if the powers do develop, then they can prove a really effective way of learning about other worlds and levels of consciousness. It is really a training in the mysteries so revered by peoples of older times.

The slow-path traveller, the complete-path traveller, respects the views of other people. He has greater tolerance and compassion for the different methods that people choose to use in their quest for freedom from suffering. He knows a great deal about the workings of the world in the relative sphere. Knowing

---

[8] Cankers (*āsava*): four pollutants, stains, taints, corruptions of mind. They are: the canker of sense desire; the canker of wishing to become better or different; the canker of views or opinions; the canker of ignorance (of the truth of things as they are).

about *kamma* and *vipāka*, action and resultant[9], he understands the kind of results you are likely to reap from specific activities like resentment and loving-kindness. With that understanding he likes to practise loving-kindness and compassion and experiences for himself their results. The complete-path traveller does everything he can to curb impatience. He cherishes fellow-travellers and quite often develops the capacity to teach others.

I say again that these descriptions are, of necessity, caricatures. There are points I could emphasise and many I have missed. I am trying to give you a flavour of two very different approaches to climbing the mountain.

☆ ☆ ☆

What path should you choose? All the major varieties of Buddhism contain both direct and complete paths, so the choice of Theravada, Mahayana or Zen really depends upon personal temperament. Whichever school you prefer, you still have to choose the direct or the complete path within that subset of Buddhism.

If you choose the faster, direct path, then you may realise enlightenment but you are unlikely to experience much ease of living here and now. The world will unquestionably be better off for the reduction in ignorance, craving and hatred that is enlightenment, but it will have little or nothing added to it by way of love, compassion, mundane wisdom and simple caring for others.

In my view, based on experience and with heart-felt endorsement of the Buddha's preference, it is better to choose the more thorough, complete path. It is better to choose the way of development that leaves a rounded, compassionate, intelligent, knowledgeable and competent enlightened being. Not only is such a being of more real value to the world after he is enlightened (I quote as an example the Buddha himself), he is also a source of harmony and well-being during his training. In every sense, he – or she – is a great fund of merit for the world.

My recommendation every time would be an unqualified vote for the complete path.

---

[9] *Kamma* and *vipāka*, action and resultant: the law of *kamma* (*karma*) which states that deliberate ethical actions have results. Broadly speaking, selfish actions lead to painful results for the perpetrator; unselfish actions lead to pleasant results.

2

NIBBANA IS
CLOSER THAN YOU THINK

At one extreme, Buddhism is practised as a religion with many beautiful ceremonies, chants and rituals. At the other, it is studied as an intellectual exercise. Until recent decades, the West always sought to understand Buddhism using intellect alone, although this happens much less now than it did. In both extreme cases, people do not expect the Teaching of the Buddha to do much for them personally; they do not believe it has much bearing on their day-to-day lives.

In those countries where Buddhism is the national religion, the Buddha is commonly regarded as God; people pray to him. The majority see Buddhism as a set of rituals presided over by monks, Buddhist 'priests'. The ordinary lay person believes that he cannot really hope to practise the Teaching, except to keep the precepts when possible. He may seek ordination for three months, but does not believe he has the capacity for meditation in depth.

In Britain it is the case, just as in places like Thailand, that some who call themselves Buddhist believe the Teaching of the Buddha has very little relevance to their day-to-day lives. They do not think it connects with anything meaningful in what they do, or what they hope for. They regard enlightenment as something impossibly distant, even unattainable. If you ask them directly, they may say that they regard enlightenment as attainable only by Buddhas – once in an aeon or two, and then only with extreme difficulty.

They say that, on that basis, surely no one today could be enlightened, and therefore it is useless to work too hard at the Teaching for – the goal being so distant and so impossible – there is really not much point. I stress that this view is held even in Buddhist countries; it does not just obtain in the West.

Yet these same people think, quite rightly, that there has to be something very valuable in the teachings of the Buddha, if only they could see what it is. In the East there is often much faith, leading people to accept what they are told and to live happily as a result. As Western values encroach on traditional teachings, however, this is becoming unfashionable. Intellectual rigour is prized more highly and faith is falling out of fashion.

In one well-known monastery in Thailand I was invited to attend an abhidhamma class, a class studying the 'higher teachings' of Buddhism. It became very quickly apparent that the teacher's objective was to get into the most abstruse intellectual detail possible – well beyond that necessary for effective meditation practice. The teacher and the students seemed to me completely to have lost sight of the main point of the Teaching, which is to discover how, practically, to come to the cessation of suffering, *nibbāna* (Sanskrit: *nirvāna*).

At one extreme we have religion, at the other extreme we have intellectuality. Neither of these is necessary to the task of coming to the cessation of suffering. You could even say that to a certain extent they are unwise. What the Buddha taught was a middle path between all extremes. I want to show you tonight that the Teaching **does** relate – in a very real and immediate way – to the lives of every one of us.

Enlightenment is available. It is immediately available, if you know where to look. In the Pali Canon (the collected works of the Buddha's Teaching in the Theravada school) there is a set of books called the *Middle Length Sayings*. These books are well worth studying, if you can persevere with the slightly archaic language and style, which does put some people off at first. In the very first discourse the Buddha speaks of the 'uninstructed average worldling' who 'recognises *nibbāna* as *nibbāna*'. He also says that the uninstructed average worldling (the 'man in the street') 'rejoices in *nibbāna*'. So *nibbāna* is not something foreign. *Nibbāna* is not something greatly removed from everybody's experience.

Let us look for a moment at the Buddha's Teaching. The central theme is that there is suffering in the world – a truth that is undeniable. There is a cause of that suffering, craving, and it is in fact possible totally to eradicate suffering by the elimination of that same craving. This elimination of suffering, frustration and distress is called *nibbāna*, which literally means 'a blowing out', a blowing out of the fires of craving and hatred. Not only does the

Buddha's Teaching state that freedom from suffering exists, it also describes a definite and systematic path to this ending of suffering and distress.

The goal of the Buddhist path, enlightenment or *nibbāna*, is the cessation of suffering. When all craving has been eradicated, never more to arise, that is the final and complete end of distress, that is enlightenment. It is enlightenment in the sense of being lightened of a burden that you have been carrying around for a long, long time.

There are two basic states of being which are common for all people, everywhere, at any stage of development. There is suffering and there is freedom from suffering. Everybody knows both. On the one hand we have craving and suffering, with which we are all completely familiar. On the other hand, we have *nibbāna* – a state completely free from suffering, frustration and distress, with which we are also familiar, although we may not have identified it clearly and most certainly do not realise that it is the goal of the Buddhist path.

The whole complex of craving and suffering is called *samsāra*, or the wheel of birth and death. It is driven by craving. That craving is based in ignorance of the way things are in reality, and when that craving stops, we can say that *samsāra*, the wheel of birth and death, also stops – thereby making visible the *nibbāna* that has always been there, obscured by the constant action of craving and hatred.

Samsāra is usually thought of as continual death and rebirth from life to life over aeons of time. But whenever craving is present – even for a moment – that is *samsāra*, that is the wheel of birth and death. Whenever craving ceases, even for a moment, that is *nibbāna*, even though it is only momentary.

That might lead one to suppose that *nibbāna* is transient, when all the books and all the teachers say that it is not. In fact, *nibbāna* never changes. It is merely uncovered, for a shorter or longer time, when craving disappears. Final enlightenment, the end of the Buddhist path, is when craving never arises again. In other words, at that point the condition on which craving arises has been eradicated so that craving itself can never again appear.

Let me recap. Every time craving arises, that is *samsāra* – the round of suffering, the round of birth and death. Every time craving ceases that is (temporary) *nibbāna*, the cessation of suffering. This 'temporary *nibbāna*' is no different in essence from the final enlightenment that is the goal of the Buddhist way. Before learning to meditate and while under training, everyone can and does experience *nibbāna* many, many times. It is impossible at that stage to avoid getting sucked back into the swamp of craving, hatred, ignorance and confusion. Full enlightenment comes when you have learned enough about the world, about mind and body, for craving never again to arise. You could call that *nibbāna* without end.

That leads us to several essential questions: When can we be aware of *nibbāna*? What is it? How do we extend our awareness of it? How do we ensure craving never arises again in future?

When can we be aware of *nibbāna*? *Nibbāna* is present when there is no craving or hatred in the mind. This state is not a mystery. It is not foreign to us. It certainly is not unattainable. It is not even unusual. It is there often, but we fail to understand what it is. Whenever a desire is satisfied, there follows immediately a state with no craving, with no desire. That state has the same stamp as enlightenment. All frustration, all suffering has vanished, at least for the time being.

Let me give you some examples. Say you have been out shopping on a summer's day. You feel grimy and sticky, hot and uncomfortable. Reaching home, you can think of nothing more attractive than a bath. So you have a bath. What happens? You feel wonderful. All the griminess and stickiness has gone. You no longer have the desire for a bath. You are washed clean, in more than one way, for at that time – although very briefly – craving has disappeared.

If you are tired and thirsty, you may crave to sit down and have a cup of tea. When you achieve your desire – to drink the tea – you feel a sense of relief, a sense of freedom from distress. It is so ordinary that you do not really take much notice of it.

You can extend that principle as widely as you like. It follows every time. Although it seems as if *nibbāna* were being created by the satisfaction of a craving, that is not so. It is the temporary cessation of the craving – not the indulgence of it – that allows the briefest of glimpses of *nibbāna*, which is ever here and now.

There is a very real problem with the satisfaction of sensual desire. No matter how often you choose to satisfy a desire, it always returns. Attempts to prolong the satisfaction, the bliss you might feel by indulging a sensual craving, are **always** short-circuited by the arising of more and stronger desires. We condition ourselves by repeated indulgence to **more** dissatisfaction, more suffering, not less. This is true not only of desire for objects of the five physical senses, but also of desire or craving for things of the mind. It is craving – of any kind, even for enlightenment itself – that is the foundation for suffering.

Indulgence never works. You can see that just by looking around. It is not very surprising. Think of people who have intense cravings for tastes. Their desire leads them to eat a lot and often become very fat. They eat, and eat, and eat; get enormous in size and find that their craving for tastes and fine foods has not in any way diminished. It has grown, and grown again, and such individuals may become completely disenchanted with the 'side-effects' of their indulgence. Their suffering increases, rather than decreases. When craving is so strong it is very difficult to control, to restrain, and people usually try instead to control the side-effects, rather than tackle the main problem. In cases of gross obesity, tackling the side-effects may mean electing for lipo-suction: having the excess fat vacuumed out of the body to return it to a more normal size.

Indulgence never works. Most people enjoy going out shopping from time to time. A spending spree now and then probably never hurt anyone very much, but to make it into a habit (and some do) can get you into very serious trouble. To indulge the sensory craving to acquire an object, far from producing a sense of satisfaction and quiet freedom from the urge to acquire, actually exacerbates it. It gets worse and worse, stronger and stronger, until people find their lives in ruins. To attack credit companies for offering easy credit is beside the point. The real problem lies in the individual refusal to restrain craving.

How can we get the awareness of *nibbāna* to last? How can we get freedom from craving and freedom from suffering to last? The satisfaction of a craving leaves a 'hole' through which *nibbāna* is momentarily visible, but further indulgence is self-defeating, for it strengthens craving. We have to look in another direction. Instead of satisfying a desire, we have to weaken it, to get rid of it. We have to forego immediate satisfaction for a future benefit.

Human beings are often addicted to sensual pleasures, eating being an obvious example. Such addiction really is in principle no different from being addicted to heroin, or to smoking cigarettes. To reduce the amount of craving for sensual things, to reduce the amount of suffering involved in such craving (in other words, to increase the amount of *nibbāna* you experience), you have to restrain desire.

Equally, human beings are often addicted to mental pleasures and pursuits. The object of their cravings is not a cream cake, a new gadget or piece of clothing. Instead they crave for justice, equality and world peace, or pleasure gained through the complexities of mathematics or philosophy. They crave to indulge in these matters just as much as someone who believes that life would not be complete without a bottle of champagne. These cravings too give rise to suffering. They too need restraining if suffering is to be reduced.

Whatever craving we wish to restrain, the principle is the same. Consider the process of giving up smoking. When you decide to give up smoking, you are within a very short time assailed by the strongest urge to have a cigarette. It strikes as a demanding, physical craving. Often, you wonder how you can resist it. The craving to smoke again can strike within ten minutes of making the decision to give up, though for most people it probably takes a few hours.

To give up smoking you have to recognise that the urge to smoke does not **have** to be indulged; it can be restrained. The sensual craving can be fought; it does not have inevitably to lead to the action of smoking. You find yourself in a fierce battle for freedom – but how long does it last? This fight for freedom lasts only about ninety seconds, no longer. After ninety seconds you find that almost overwhelming craving suddenly disappears as though it had never existed. You are free from it for another few hours, or for a few days. Then another strong craving arises and you have another extremely fraught battle on your hands – for ninety seconds. Then that craving goes away and you are at peace until the next time.

Repeating this process you find – gradually, gradually – that the craving, the urge, begins to diminish. It is not as strong as it was; it is easier to handle. The urge comes less frequently, so your moments of (as it were) *nibbāna*, periods when that craving is absent, get longer and longer. Ultimately, you are not thinking about, or craving for, a cigarette for days and days, maybe weeks at a time, although you may dream about it. As your restraint continues, you do not experience any problem for months at a time. Occasionally, after a meal, you may be surprised to find yourself thinking, 'Oh, I would really like a cigarette!' By this time, though, there is not much force behind the thought, so you resist easily, the battle won and the war almost over.

The one thing that completely undermines resolutions to restrain craving is drinking alcohol. Alcohol can dissolve resolutions with lightning speed. I have seen a man who had 'given up smoking' with four cigarettes burning at the same time. After a few drinks, his inhibitions relaxed, and he was unable to hold on to his resolve. He lit one cigarette, placed it in the ashtray and forgot it, lit another and another until there were four. He had quickly fallen back into his old pattern, for he no longer had the will to restrain the craving.

☆ ☆ ☆

Giving up smoking is one thing, and you may think that it is a special case. But restraint can be applied in exactly the same way to any kind of craving you can think of. Not only can you give up smoking, you can give up just about anything you choose. Taken to the extreme, restraint becomes asceticism. You give up all luxuries. You abandon all creature comforts. You give up almost everything that makes one normally human and lead a life of the utmost austerity. You may even introduce painful practices like flagellation to further reduce your craving for sensual comfort.

Men and women sometimes try heroically to eliminate craving by sheer will-power and control. They deny themselves everything but those things absolutely necessary to maintain physical existence. In this, they completely overlook the fact that the craving to deny themselves things is still very much a craving – and thus an indulgence of the very problem they are trying to overcome.

I once knew a meditator who illustrated this problem very well. He was sincere, an extremely hard worker, and he was determined to conquer craving. He gave up smoking, sensibly enough, in view of what was known even then about smoking as a cause of cancer and lung disease. Realising that his drinking was perhaps a little indulgent, he gave up wine. He then became worried about an area of sensual indulgence that everybody thinks of a lot but seldom mentions: sex. He gave up sleeping with his wife. He believed, wrongly, that this normal married activity was not appropriate when attempting to pursue the meditative path. He did not accept that, as a lay man, he was free to conduct a sexual relationship.

It looked very much as though he was going to give up life altogether. He was convinced that giving up, cutting off, extreme control, was the right way to approach the goal of this Teaching. Much of his action was rooted in hatred and it was difficult to persuade him that he needed to moderate his behaviour, to find a middle path. I think it was only when his wife slashed all his best suits and shoes to ribbons, and then left him, that he realised he might have a problem. He could have avoided much of his difficulty by recognising that he needed to restrain **all** cravings, including the craving to control. Such restraint would assuredly have involved periods of abstention from sexual activity, on residential meditation courses, for example, but most probably not the breakdown of his marriage.

On a residential course, free from all the distractions of the world, the mind can be trained for insight into the truth of things as they are. Ultimately, it is **insight** that removes the basis for craving and hatred. No amount of restraint or control can ever be completely successful. Total restraint is only a means to an end and is applied in the very short term to overcome a particular problem. It is not the goal of the Buddhist path, nor does it lead to that goal.

Buddha Dhamma, the Teaching of the Buddhas, is a middle path. It is a path between the extremes of sensual indulgence and self-mortification. Of course, sometimes it is very difficult to know just where the middle lies. That is why it is essential to have a teacher.

It is difficult to find the middle. The Buddha himself spent twenty-nine years as a rich and pampered prince. He knew luxury like most of us never will. Throwing that aside, he sought freedom from suffering in the opposite extreme. He practised the strictest kind of asceticism for about six years, sometimes living only on one grain of rice a day, suffering the most terrible austerities.

He found, though, that it was not any good; severe asceticism merely weakened the body and dulled the mind. In the end he opted for what we know, today, as the middle path between those extremes. You take sufficient food to keep you healthy, sufficient exercise to keep the body functioning. You do not overdo it. You do not underdo it. Although heavily censured when he turned away from asceticism, it became quickly apparent that the Buddha's then revolutionary approach was a wise one.

When you are run down, your states of mind become less happy, less joyful than is otherwise the case. One's state of mind does depend very much on physical well-being. Most people find that if they are extremely tired, they get bad-tempered and irritable. Those trained in the meditative way find instead that when debilitated they experience life with equanimity, but without joy. To experience joy in living, you have to be fit and healthy. You need to have a balanced lifestyle.

You could say, I suppose, that a balanced lifestyle is a middle path. On its own, however, it is not enough. You cannot prolong the moments when *nibbāna* is visible simply by adopting a balanced lifestyle. Desires and cravings still arise. Admittedly they are a little more subtle than the desires of a glutton or a heroin addict, but nevertheless desires arise constantly and obscure our vision of perfection.

Cravings that arise even when one's lifestyle is sensible and balanced include desires for experiencing through the senses, cravings for truth, freedom, justice, intellectual ability, concentration, mindfulness and many other mental skills.

☆ ☆ ☆

I want to look for a moment at craving for physical sense stimulation. We all, before we understand the training clearly, constantly indulge in sensory craving. That indulgence, that wallowing in the senses, prevents our momentary experiences of *nibbāna* from lasting.

You can sometimes see clear evidence of such indulgence when looking at meditators who are new to residential courses. What do they do when they come in? At the earliest opportunity they get out into the gardens, and they look long and hard, searchingly, at everything around them. They want to see what flowers are out, to admire the view, to examine the place to which they have come. If they are not particularly interested in the gardens, then they are interested in the other people on the course. Their eyes are constantly moving, searching to see who is there. They fasten avidly on every visual clue to discover who their companions are and how they are faring. They would claim to feel a lot better for having seen what is going on, whether they are interested in gardens or people. What those new to meditation often do not realise is that such indulgence in the sense of sight prevents any deeper experience. It covers it up.

The next stage in prolonging the moments of *nibbāna* is to restrain the senses. Having restrained his overall behaviour to conform to the five precepts, the meditator needs now to restrain the craving for sensory indulgence. When successful, such restraint leads to great calmness and, coupled with concentration, can even lead to the fixed meditations (*jhāna*). In any event, simply restraining the senses leads to a tremendous sense of space, calmness and freedom.

You see more experienced meditators practising such restraint impeccably. When on a residential course, they keep their eyes on the ground about fifteen paces ahead. They do not look around, they do not seek out what is going on in the garden or the environment. Restraining their interest in other people, experienced meditators try to keep themselves to themselves for as long as the retreat lasts. Success is won only with some difficulty: the desire to indulge the senses – particularly the sense of sight – is exceedingly strong and hard to combat.

Sense-restraint combined with mindfulness of body[1] can induce, within a day or two, intense peacefulness and serenity. There also arises a sense of mental and physical spaciousness that is delightful. It is a much more satisfying result than knowing whom you are sharing the course with, or what is going on in the surroundings. This deep serenity is one of the 'fruits of the life of a recluse'. Practising aloofness in this way, being a recluse – even for a few days – brings enormous benefits. Those benefits are ones that you could not have guessed at beforehand, for they can be realised only through correct practice.

When deep serenity arises, craving is suppressed and there is a greater likelihood of prolonging the periods when *nibbāna* is visible. If you practise concentration and restraint to a greater extent, you can get such periods to last longer. Some are seduced by this success into the belief that total restraint and concentration must produce permanent *nibbāna*, but it is not so:

---

[1] Mindfulness of body: setting up systematic awareness of the transience of body and bodily actions. See Chapter 7.

craving still arises – and sooner rather than later.

The path of concentration is a sidetrack. It does not work as a means of uncovering *nibbāna* permanently. Both control and pure concentration are dead ends. Although it is possible to hold desires at bay for extended periods of time using concentration, you do nothing at all to eradicate them. They are still there, walled up behind the dam of concentration. Whenever it ceases (and cease it must: you cannot concentrate indefinitely), back flood in the desires, back floods in *samsāra*, and the problems start all over again.

To arrive at final *nibbāna*, at permanent *nibbāna*, needs insight. We have to negate craving, not suppress it; we have to undercut it. To do this, we need to find out how suffering and craving arise, and dig out their very roots. This sphere of activity is the province of *vipassanā*, insight meditation, which eventually shows us that all things are utterly transient. Every feeling, every sight, every sound, every thought is transient. Whatever you examine closely with the eye of attention, of insight, you find that it lasts only for a fleeting instant. There is in reality nothing at which to grasp.

When transience is seen deeply enough, with the eye of meditation, it becomes completely impossible to persuade yourself to crave for things, to grasp at things, physical or mental. You **know** that they are changing so rapidly that they do not assume any permanent state; that anything you might look at is dissolving, even as you regard it.

You realise through insight that it is literally impossible to acquire objects. This realisation completely negates craving. Insight wisdom is the very opposite of ignorance, and destroys craving altogether. Ignorance says, 'Things are permanent, they are worth acquiring,' and it grasps and clings to objects and people, to sights and sounds. Ignorance and the resultant grasping obscure *nibbāna*, they hide freedom from us. They cover it with the murk and muck of sensual desire and all other cravings.

When craving is eliminated by wisdom, by insight, it never arises again. That leaves us with a state that we might call permanent *nibbāna*. It is the goal of the Buddhist path; it is enlightenment.

Some people believe that enlightenment is somehow an extinction; as though one falls into a black hole, never more to experience anything. They believe that enlightenment is the end of everything. Nothing could be further from the truth. The belief that when you get enlightened you disappear in a puff of blue smoke is very common, particularly in the West, simply because *nibbāna*, enlightenment, is not understood.

Enlightenment is the permanent absence of craving. It is the absence of the very ignorance that makes craving possible. Nothing else changes.

The Buddha lived for another forty-five years after his enlightenment at the age of 35. He taught up and down the length and breadth of the Ganges valley in India. He talked to people from all walks of life, ate meals, walked and slept. As he got older, he experienced pains in his back and would sit with his back to the sun, allowing the warmth to ease the pain. He led a very normal life, under the circumstances. This man who became Buddha did not disappear in a puff of blue smoke. Why should anybody else? No one questions the Buddha's attainment of enlightenment. Why should enlightenment be different for other people?

When all craving is absent, that is *nibbāna*. That is the cessation of suffering. The absence of sensory cravings does not mean that all sensory objects disappear, however. Sensory and mental objects still arise. What does not arise is craving. There is absolutely no craving for them, nor any hatred of them. There is no burning desire to acquire things, mental or physical, nor any such desire to do away with them.

Nibbāna is available to all – to everyone – here and now. There is no need to regard it as available only in the dim and distant future, as a remote possibility. *Nibbāna* is immediate, it is real and, though it seems improbable, you all know what it is. Meditation is the perfect way to bring that knowledge to the forefront of the mind. Meditation needs a great deal of work, but that work is repaid a thousandfold, a millionfold, by the discovery of the freedom that never dies.

3

HOW TRUE IS TRUTH?

The Buddha taught for forty-five years and in that time expressed his teachings in many different ways dependent upon his audience at the time. Newcomers sometimes find the variety of expression confusing and it helps to remember that the Teaching has but one objective: the complete eradication of all suffering.

The Buddha taught people from all walks of life. Some of them were young in the ways of Dhamma; others were sophisticated and philosophical. By no means all were able to become enlightened immediately. There were many whom the Buddha taught who understood virtually nothing of what he had to say. Others could understand his advice to live a sensible and moderate life but had no interest in the more philosophical teachings.

While the aim of the Teaching is single, the eradication of suffering takes place on two levels: there is the reduction of suffering in the worlds of *samsāra*, and there is the total eradication of all frustration and distress in *nibbāna*, beyond that wheel of birth and death.

The Buddha taught the way to gain most happiness and satisfaction from living in the world. He gave advice on subjects as varied as ethical conduct, relationships and how much money to put aside for a rainy day. He told people what they needed to know to get the best out of life in all its many facets. At this level there was never any question of a deeply philosophical or meditative approach to life.

The Buddha recognised that meditative analysis was a subject of interest to fewer people, for it required a subtler appreciation of the disadvantages in even the happiest of worldly circumstances. For these individuals, the Buddha taught the 'higher truth'; he taught a way leading beyond even the most sublime of worldly happinesses to an ultimate goal that surpasses anything the world has to offer. These two kinds of teaching are called the two kinds of truth or, sometimes, the two quests.

Some find it strange that there can be more than one kind of truth, but all of us are quite familiar with the idea of levels of truthfulness.

If you ask someone 'How are you?', you would probably expect him to reply 'I'm fine!', whatever his actual state of health; but you do not regard him as telling a lie because of that. You accept his statement as a kind of truth.

A friend tells you proudly that he has had the 'same' car for fifteen years. Is he telling the truth? The car has had new tyres regularly, a new engine at 60,000 miles, two new clutches, a new sub-frame assembly ... The same car?

You meet someone you have not seen for years and years. He says, 'You haven't changed a bit ...' Is he lying?

If you are house-hunting, the estate agent's details from which you make your initial selection contain a wealth of information, if only you know how to read them. What does 'Suit the discerning handyman' really mean? Or, 'Compact and easy to run'? If you want a decaying Victorian dog-kennel, you will probably be delighted. Does the estate agent's information tell the truth? Well, yes ... in a manner of speaking.

The two levels of truth in Buddha Dhamma are worldly truth and higher or ultimate truth. Worldly or mundane truth describes the operation of beings and the world in terms that nearly all can understand. However, like someone describing the 'same' car he has had for years, worldly truth may not give a 100-percent accurate picture. The higher truth, ultimate truth, describes our experience of the world in terms that are precise and provable. It avoids the errors inherent in thinking of the 'same' car or the 'same' person. Let us look at each of these in more detail.

Worldly truth is concerned with the world as we generally think of it. It describes our experience in conventional terms with respect to beings who are born and die, who act in various ways and who experience happiness and suffering.

Buddha Dhamma says that our visible, human world is but one small part of a universe that extends into regions normally inaccessible to human sight. Beyond the range of normal human senses are planes of existence that include the hell worlds, the worlds of ghosts and demons, the worlds of the terrestrial devas[1] and the worlds of the lower and higher gods. In each of these regions there are beings like ourselves, sometimes differing in shape, sometimes differing in perception, who enjoy happier or more miserable circumstances. In most cases, they are not born as we are born of mother and father, but appear spontaneously, as each of us does when experiencing a vivid dream. Their stay, whether in the happier or the more miserable realms of existence, is always temporary, although usually of longer duration than a human life.

Worldly truth describes how beings die from one plane of existence only to be born on another, higher or lower. It describes the world in a way that seems 'common sense' and speaks of a 'being' or a 'self' who is born, who lives and loves, who decays and dies. There is always the emphasis on how you, as a being-living-in-a-world, choose to act and the results of those actions. Worldly truth describes this 'endless faring on' (*samsāra*) and emphasises the fact that life is never extinguished; it goes on and on, round and round, endlessly. Death is merely a change of state, never an annihilation.

The location of a being's next birth is not random but is affected by what he has done in the past. All deliberate actions associated with the belief in a 'being' or a 'self' or a 'soul' have results that may manifest either in the very lifetime those actions are performed or later, in another lifetime.

Actions like theft or murder may lead to gaol and even death in the lifetime they were committed. They lead to poverty and disfigurement in future lives. On the other hand, free generosity leads in this very life to great gladness, friendship and many opportunities. In a future life it leads to wealth and to being born into a good or 'noble'[2] family. In short, actions done with the thought of self-profit strongly in the mind always lead to painful results and a poor rebirth. Actions done with the thought of the welfare of others uppermost in mind give beautiful results both

---

[1] Terrestrial devas: heavenly beings in circumstances happier than the human realm and normally invisible to it. These beings are still in *kāma-loka* and are therefore still beset by sensual desire (in contrast to the lower and higher gods, who are without sensual desire).

[2] Noble: in the sense of ethically beautiful. It has no direct connection with social aristocracy.

in this and in future lives.

Actions do have results. There is unquestionably a painful result of selfish action and, equally, a wonderful result of unselfish action. Unselfish action finds its culmination in a life of service to others. To serve all other beings in everything you do is the highest kind of life there is on the worldly planes.

The worldly quest is undertaken when someone, 'liable to birth, ageing, decay, dying and sorrow because of self, seeks what is also liable to birth, ageing, decay, dying and sorrow'. He seeks satisfaction anywhere in the conditioned scheme of things, within the worlds of *samsāra*.

What does it mean, 'liable to birth because of self'? It means that because someone holds the belief that a self exists, so is he or she conditioned by that belief always to seek the things that will make that self happy; and that those things are themselves 'liable to birth, ageing, decay, dying and sorrow'.

Believing in the existence of an independent self renders him 'liable to (re)birth', for with self-view arise cravings upon which rebirth depends. Such an individual seeks sensual pleasures, relationships, power, possessions and wealth, or a good rebirth among the devas, where life is easy and pleasant. In more immediate terms, he or she may seek constantly to experience pleasurable feelings, or to be always in the right and praised for it. He may crave to be honoured and respected and never to be slighted or abused; he may wish to be rich, to own many possessions, or to be famous and powerful. These are the objects of the worldly quest. These are the things that are liable to change; to 'birth, ageing, decay, dying and sorrow'. It is the view of self that provides the attachment to *samsāra*. Self-view ensures that the individual never breaks free, never finds the happiness, satisfaction and incomparable security that he or she really seeks.

The average, untrained person does not know 'things as they are'. He firmly believes that the things of the world can provide happiness and satisfaction, in spite of all the evidence to the contrary. The average, untrained person takes no notice of the words of those who have overcome craving and attachment. He knows nothing of Dhamma and is bound by six particular views of self. These views tie the individual to the wheel of rebirth and suffering with bonds stronger than steel.

When considering the body, made of flesh and blood and affording him pleasure and pain, he thinks, 'This is my body' or he thinks, 'I am this body' or he thinks, 'This body is my self.' Such a person will be greatly concerned with the state of the body. He or she may be fanatical about diet, physical fitness or good looks. There may be considerable vanity or cowardice on the one hand or extreme foolhardiness and great feats of strength on the other.

When considering a feeling, pleasant or unpleasant, the worldly person thinks, 'This is my feeling, I am this feeling, this feeling is my self.' Many a person identifies with feeling, believes feeling to be the core of his or her being. They work hard always to remove unpleasant feelings and to get pleasant ones. In the process they are completely caught up in worldly concerns. They bind themselves to the wheel of *samsāra* and create for themselves by their actions in the present the certainty of future distress.

When considering a perception, whether pleasant or unpleasant, he thinks, 'This is my perception, I am this, this is my self.' This is another common area of identification, particularly with perception in the form of memory. Many identify with memory and in consequence experience suffering, whether the memories are pleasant or unpleasant.

When considering a volitional tendency, a habitual action, he thinks, 'This is mine, I am this, this is my self.' Volitional tendencies are things like being quick to take offence, always criticising others and experiencing intense longings to possess certain things or people. Such habitual activities of mind can be efficient or inefficient, unselfish or selfish. Identifying with volitional tendencies is something you see often in those who are, on the face of it, working to better themselves. Always do they identify with tendencies like hatred and lust that arise in mind, thinking that they are in some way themselves. For this kind of person the common cry is, 'I am such a bad person (self), to do these things.' He or she makes the mistake of believing that the action – or the tendency to it – is somehow the 'real self'.

When considering consciousness, whether low or exalted, he thinks, 'This is my consciousness, I am this consciousness, this consciousness is my self.' In this case, someone thinks that his thoughts, his states of mind and his awareness are his 'real self'. He cannot accept the fact that all these are changing, transient experiences that cannot be the self-that-never-changes.

In every case there is a mistaken view of self, of identity or ownership, which inevitably leads to suffering and sorrow. Body, feelings, perceptions, volitional actions and consciousness are all fleeting, ephemeral – and what does not last cannot be the self.

It does not stop there, however, for apart from considering his personal makeup in this way, the untrained individual also applies similar wrong view to external objects. When considering a sense object, whether pleasant or unpleasant, he thinks, 'This is mine, I am this, this is my self.'

A woman felt safe and well only when inside her beautifully and artistically decorated apartment. If ever she had to go out, she suffered dreadfully from the crudity and coarseness of the external world and felt under attack. She believed that the contents of her living space were, in some real way, her self – and paid the price for that identification.

Because the average, untrained person thinks these thoughts, always in terms of self, he is not free from suffering. He is beset on all sides with problems and can never free himself from the tangle of views that is *samsāra*. He fares on and on, round and round the cycle of births and deaths, with no end in sight.

With considerable pain and some intelligence, a person ceases to be fascinated and trapped by this merry-go-round of suffering; he starts to look for an escape from these unsatisfactory conditions. He has become someone who, 'liable to birth, ageing, decay, dying and sorrow, having known the peril in what is liable to birth, ageing, decay, dying and sorrow, seeks the unborn, the unageing, the undecaying, the undying, the uttermost security from the bonds that is *nibbāna*'.

This kind of person is disenchanted with the things of the world. Bored by the search for wealth and possessions, for example, he cannot see any point in striving for them. He knows that they cannot make him happy, though they may provide comfort for a brief while. He knows that the satisfaction they do provide is empty and pointless, that it is not ultimately worthwhile. He draws ever closer to the noble quest.

You are on the noble quest when you see the peril in things of the world – that they are all liable to birth, ageing, decay, death and sorrow – and turn from them to seek the undying, the sorrowless that is *nibbāna*. Then you cease always to seek only pleasant feelings, or to experience praise and never to be blamed. It is then that you cease to wish always to have your worth recognised by others.

The bridge between the worldly quest and the noble quest is a bridge of truth. Worldly truth describes the world in an obvious way and is ideal for gaining as much happiness as is possible in the world. Noble or ultimate truth is very much more precise and analytical. It is a tool with which to transcend the limitations of the worldly view by removing confusion and blindness. It is a tool that can set your feet firmly on the noble path.

Ultimate truth goes beyond the conventional truth we have looked at so far. Ultimate truth transcends the idea of people dying, and being reborn; it goes beyond ideas of persons, selves and the like. Dealing with the 'building blocks' of experience, it says that at the most fundamental level there are only fleeting mental and physical phenomena. These momentary elements of experience are changing all the time, flashing into existence and out of existence continuously. When life is examined closely there is to be found no self, no being, to be born or to die. All is conditioned, and there is within it nothing permanent. There is no 'self'. There is nothing of the nature of 'self'. There is no 'one' to own any 'thing'. There are simply conditions arising and passing away, with great rapidity.

Ultimate truth is not a theory, but a description of fact. Something that can be tested and proven through observation, it differs from Western science in that it includes the mind and mental factors. It is therefore comprehensive in a way that science, as it stands, can never be.

☆ ☆ ☆

The Buddha would ask seekers, 'Is the body permanent or impermanent?' Everyone knows that the body decays and dies, usually this side of one hundred years; it is undeniably impermanent.

He would ask, 'Is what is impermanent painful or pleasant?'

They would reply, 'Painful,' for anything that decays cannot be a basis for true happiness, for true security from life's ills.

The Buddha would then ask, 'But is it fitting to regard that which is impermanent, painful, liable to change as "This is mine, I am this, this is my self"?'

The answer is a definite no. It is not fitting to regard the impermanent, the painful as the self. The self is, by definition, a permanent and unchanging entity. Moreover, considering the comprehensive analysis of every aspect of experience covered by 'body, feeling, perceptions, volitional tendencies, consciousness and all sense objects', it is definitely 'not fitting' to regard any of the elements of mind and body as having anything to do with a self: they are all non-self (*anattā*).

The Buddha used to ask his monks, 'Monks, could you take hold of some possession, the possession of which would be permanent, unchanging, undecaying, undying and lasting as to the eternal?' They replied that there is no possession conceivable that could last in this way. All possession is transient: either the possession itself decays and disappears or the possessor does, through death if nothing else. If there is the least grasping or attachment to a possession there will be sorrow and lamentation at the change.

The Buddha would then ask, 'Monks, could you grasp that grasping of the theory of self, so that by grasping that theory of self there would not arise grief, sorrow, lamentation and despair?' Again the monks replied that they could not. Grasping at the idea of a permanent, unchanging self is bound to lead to distress of the worst kind, for nowhere within mind and body on any level of existence can be found anything that lasts for even a second.

Sometimes people claim that the self or soul is really outside all our experience, outside all the worlds of the universe, that it is somehow separate. They say that the self is not to be found in the hell states, the ghost realms, the human and terrestrial deva realms or even in the realms of the lower and higher gods. They say that the self is somehow apart from body, feelings, perceptions, volitional tendencies, consciousness and all sense and thought objects. To these people the Buddha said, 'If self and what belongs to self, although actually existing, are incomprehensible, is not the view that "After dying I will become permanent, unchanging, steadfast like unto the eternal", is not this view absolute and complete folly?' In other words, if a self (soul) is not now and can never be knowable or comprehensible, in this world or the next, then to believe in its existence is complete foolishness.

The noble quest turns away from the things of the world and from all identification with self. Someone on the noble quest is disenchanted with what the world has to offer, either in this life or the next. He or she seeks that release from dissatisfaction and sorrow that is to be found elsewhere, outside the realms of the conditioned and the relative. Only outside, beyond, *samsāra* can there be any hope of true happiness and satisfaction. Only outside the transient and the unsatisfactory can there be found any measure of true peace.

The noble quest is, in a way, an extension of the positive side of the worldly quest. On the worldly quest, it becomes clear that the way to happiness in the world lies in the eradication of self-importance through service to others. In a similar manner, success on the noble quest rests upon the overcoming of the view of self, on reducing self-importance further still. If true release is to be found, unselfishness has to develop so that any belief in a self is destroyed.

Those who go beyond *samsāra*, who escape totally from the death-grip of the limited and conditioned, are few in any one generation, but they do exist. Some find their liberation through the teachings, preserved in the great religious movements of the world, of men and women of historical time. Others find their way to truth through more secret doctrines. In every case, no matter what way they have chosen to follow, they have to meet face to face with one who is liberated. They have to take instruction from a man or a woman who **knows**, who has 'gone beyond', who has destroyed the fetters that bind the individual to the wheel of birth and death, to the wheel of suffering. Only in this way can someone get adequate instruction and adequate training.

To read the books on your own is never enough; it never has been and it never will be. To become expert at the intellectual intricacies of the recorded teachings, yet to fail to seek for and to listen to one who is freed, is to waste your time. With a minute number of exceptions, all beings have to learn the way to the beyond from someone who knows what and where it is.

Someone who has found such a teacher centres his life in an approach to the things of the world completely different from those on the quest for worldly satisfaction and happiness. He recognises the danger in a life devoted to the idea of self, however subtle. Such an individual regards the world in a way that seems like madness to the average, uninstructed person.

The seeker on the noble quest, when he considers the body with all its pleasures and pains, says, 'This is not my body, I am not this body, this body is not my self.' If he suffers bodily illness he does not moan and complain about his lot but says, 'I am not this, this is not mine, this is not my self.' If he has to have a tooth out he does not fall into depression about this assault on his physical integrity but thinks, 'I am not this, this is not mine, this is not my self.'

An instructed disciple deals with feeling in the same way, always seeking to avoid identifying with it. If painful mental feelings arise through being rejected in a relationship, say, there is no falling into self-pity and sorrow. The meditator in training refuses to be swept away by attachment and always attempts to look upon the morass of distressing feeling and say, 'This is not mine, I am not this, this is not my self.'

A meditator under instruction attempts always to train himself in this way with respect to every division of mind and body, internal and external, past, present and future, leaving nothing out. No matter what arises he refuses to fall into the trap of self-oriented thinking.

The instructed meditator applies the same kind of thinking to all external objects. If he should find himself caught up in craving for a new gadget, for new clothes or for the holiday of a lifetime, he will say of these things, 'I am not this, this is not mine, this is not my self.'

With diligent practice and systematic application, the meditator will eventually realise the goal for which people take up the life of meditation. He or she will come to know what has to be known and do what has to be done. In the knowing, he will come to see that there is no self within the worlds of *samsāra*, and that *nibbāna* also does not contain any form of self. Truly the myth of self is the one consistent thing that keeps beings bound to the wheel of suffering. Get rid of the view of self and you get rid of the world of birth and death. Then you come to see that there never was a self in the first place: it was merely blindness and ignorance that had prevented true seeing of what is really there.

It is a little like having lived all your life in a dark cave, never being sure where the walls, the ceiling or the exits were, never being sure of the real shape of the space around you. When at last you bring in some light to the darkness, immediately your old idea of the cave disappears. The illumination of true vision eliminates what had been total darkness, including all your speculations about the reality of the cave. When this occurs, there is never any need to refer to your earlier idea of how things were; it simply becomes irrelevant. Now you know things as they are. What interest can speculative fantasies have for you now?

4

GREAT EXPECTATIONS

The Teaching of the Buddha is a vast and complex subject; its scope is enormous, ranging across all the worlds and covering in detail the development of mental skills rarely even dreamed of. Even so, it can be summarised in a few words. The Buddha himself encapsulated his entire Teaching in four noble truths. These outline the problem we face, the reason for its existence, the resolution of the problem and the method to realise that solution.

He said, 'There is suffering, distress, in the world.' 'Suffering' (*dukkha*) includes distress of every kind, physical and mental. It includes the frustration at not being able to answer why things are the way they are. It is undeniable: there is suffering in the world. He said, too, 'There is a definite reason for this. There is a cause of suffering.' That cause is craving, wanting things to be different than they are. Suffering is not something capricious. It arises dependent upon an identifiable cause.

In the third truth, the Buddha stated, 'There is, without question, a cessation of suffering. There is a state beyond the world of suffering.' He said that anyone could come to the beyond, to the complete eradication of suffering and distress, by eradicating the craving upon which it depends, the craving for things to be different than they are.

Lastly, and of singular interest, is the fourth truth. The Buddha said, 'There is an actual, defined pathway, a way of practice that leads to the complete cessation of suffering and distress.' Through correct practice of this way, the eightfold path, one can come to the eradication of craving, by eliminating the ignorance necessary for craving to exist. One can attain to the final goal of the Buddha's Teaching, enlightenment itself, the total ending of all suffering and distress.

The fourth truth tells us that there is a defined path that, when followed, will bring the practitioner to the eradication of all suffering. That path is the eightfold path, the first factor of which is right view. It is right view that concerns me specifically this evening. I want to give you some idea of what is covered by the term 'view' in its various aspects, right and wrong.

Right view is often misunderstood. People think that it means only getting one's ideas straight. They believe that they have only to do some study, and that is enough. Study is part of it; one does have to get one's ideas straight, but there is far more to it. There is far more to right view than mere intellectual belief. To develop right view is to come to perceive the world in a new and radically different way, based on direct observation of real life. There is a vast difference between the views you might get secondhand from studying books, and views acquired by directly experiencing what life is and what life does. In the first case you have theory; in the second, wisdom.

Right view is in many ways as much a matter of feeling as thinking, for how we feel about matters has a very direct bearing on how we act. The Buddha himself said, 'That which you feel, you perceive; that which you perceive, you are conscious of.' He said also, 'It is difficult to separate these three – feeling, perception and consciousness.' It takes a great deal of careful, practical discrimination to do so.

The views we hold affect our lives. They affect our lives whether those views are true or whether they are false. Views produce for us expectations, for a view is a belief or expectation about things. Right view aligns our expectations with what is possible in reality. Wrong views ensure that our expectations are unrealistic and produce frustration and distress.

If views are right, then life is comfortable, exciting, bright and interesting, and there are not too many dreadful surprises. If views are wrong, then there are all kinds of shocks in store. All views, no matter what they are, have an effect. Our ideas, our beliefs, affect absolutely everything we do – from the way we dress to the way we eat; from the way we talk to the way we think; from the way we relate to others to whether or not we are happy with our own company in solitude.

As well as right and wrong, we can look at views in another way: as conscious and unconscious. Conscious views include views, beliefs, opinions or conclusions that stem from direct observation. In these cases you are aware of the opinion you hold. For example, you might have been to an Italian restaurant a few times and found it to serve palatable food in pleasant surroundings. You have the view that it is a good restaurant; you believe that to be so. You expect that when you go in there next time, you will again be served decent food in a pleasant setting.

Conscious views can be changed by experience or by gaining new information. Say the Italian restaurant comes under new management. You eat there a couple of times and realise the standard has fallen off. Your expectations change accordingly. Your actions change accordingly: you no longer go there; you seek out another place. All this activity is based on conscious views, conscious opinions, formed by living in the real world.

Such views influence our expectations on the conscious level and, assuming the views to be accurate, that is fine. What happens when we get hold of wrong information, though? We may have expectations that are wrong, in the sense of being unrealisable. How often have you been told, 'Oh, you'll like so-and-so – he's really a very nice person.' You meet him, and find that you do not take to him at all. On the other hand, someone may say, 'Watch out for so-and-so – he has a really dreadful temper.' You meet him, only to find him quite charming and very good company. Your expectations have been confounded, because the information you were given was inaccurate. Your view was wrong.

Conscious views quite definitely influence our expectations – often more than we realise – but not nearly as strongly as unconscious views. Unconscious views are very different. They exist, and are acted upon, without any awareness. Being invisible, they act very much more powerfully. For most of us, much of our behaviour is governed by things of which we are not conscious. We do not even know that we hold expectations of a particular kind. We are definitely not aware that those expectations are influencing our behaviour in any way.

Accepting an opinion as a fact, we may never think to test its accuracy. Maybe we read something in a newspaper or a book, or hear it on the television or radio news, and believe it implicitly, never dreaming that it may be untrue. Without personal experience we have only someone's unsupported word on which to form the opinion. This is **not** a problem if the information is accurate – although it is still an opinion, a view, and not something we know for ourselves by experience. The whole matter is more worrying if you consider that 'news' may be distorted deliberately, for political motives. How accurate are our views of reality then?

Another way of developing unconscious views is by absorbing them in childhood. Many opinions, attitudes and expectations are conditioned very early in life. Sometimes those expectations are related to childhood things, but are carried through to our middle years where they may no longer be appropriate. If you see a five-year-old going to bed with a teddy-bear, you think that it is a very natural thing to do. If you see a forty-five-year-old going to bed with a teddy-bear, you begin to wonder if he is a little strange. We have to let go of childhood patterns of behaviour – including views – if we are successfully to grow.

Unless we change, unless we let go of expectations that are no longer right, we can find ourselves acting in some very strange and inappropriate ways. Views influence our actions in all spheres of life – and actions have results. Many unconscious views and expectations can be damaging. For example, unconsciously, we may expect that strangers are dangerous, that black is evil, that white is good, that the world is a dangerous place, that people will get you unless you get them first. We may believe that life should be fair, though our definition of 'fair' is based entirely upon our own perceived advantage and has little or no relation to our actions. With such views and expectations come actions that lead inexorably to all kinds of distress.

If we have wrong views and expectations, then we often act in ways that are detrimental to ourselves and to other people. Let me describe some common expectations found in the West today, and see what you make of them. These views may be conscious, or unconscious, depending upon who holds them. Some people will understand and recognise the views quite clearly, and others – never having given them a moment's thought – will be unaware of their existence and thus unaware of the motivation for much of their behaviour.

Western science today believes that we have only one lifetime. This is in contrast to probably most of the world's population, which believes that we have many, many lifetimes. People holding the Western scientific view would expect never to consider future-life results of their actions. If, as they believe, there is only one life, there is clearly no point in planning for a future one. Thus long-term ethics, long-term morality as some might prefer to call it, is rendered invalid and useless; it can hold no interest. The only thing that really matters, given this view, is not getting caught. A single view can affect the ethics of an entire culture.

Science, and medicine too, treat the mind as if it does not exist. If you ask an orthodox doctor about the cause of a disease or illness, and suggest to him that it might be based on mental stress, he will pooh-pooh the idea. The medical establishment is willing to concede that stress might be a contributing factor, but insists that the real cause of a disease must be physical or chemical. Commonly, doctors do not know the cause of an ailment and yet still believe that there must be a physical cause. They 'know' that mind does not have any part to play. It is, they believe, itself an effect and therefore can produce nothing further. Point out that the argument is circular and you get nowhere at all.

The view that mind does not really exist has surprising ramifications. It leads to the expectation that there must be not only a physical cause for disease but also a physical cure. Further, the view leads to the belief that there must always be a physical cause for dis-ease, for unhappiness, and a consequent material cure for that, too. This view, so widespread in the West, leads to the expectation that the cure for unhappiness is to be found in the acquisition of more and more material things, in a higher and higher standard of living. It follows directly from the original view.

Psychiatry and psychology have gone a little further. They agree that both mind and body are necessary to life. There is, however, a distinct lack of clarity about the function of mental action and its results. Usually there is no real belief that mental action can have **any** results. They believe that something you do only in your mind cannot affect the 'real world'. They therefore do not see a need to act in an ethical way on the mental level, for they believe that it is not going to make any difference anyway.

All beliefs lead to expectations that govern the way we approach every aspect of our lives. Scientists cannot conceive of a mental universe, so cannot entertain the idea of something beyond the mind, whether God or *nibbāna* or anything else. Those subscribing to the rational, materialistic, scientific view of the universe find themselves unable to admit the possibility of modes of existence other than the material. They are in greater difficulties still when it comes to the existence of something that transcends even non-material states of being.

Do you see what that means? Given the definitions adhered to by science, materialism and medicine, it means that anyone who has a religious outlook on life must be deluded, or at least addicted to fantasy. Similarly, normal, sane people are those who believe that there is only one life, who believe that the mind has no reality, and that the answer to suffering lies in amassing material goods. I am simplifying the subject, I know, but you can see that these views affect every one of us – directly or indirectly.

If you expect to find happiness with the accumulation of material goods, you expect the impossible. Happiness does not result from the accumulation of things; it is not possible to find happiness in what is impermanent, unsatisfactory and non-self. In the West we subscribe to an entire set of wrong views by believing that the self can find lasting happiness in the ordinary, work-a-day world. These are the wrong views of permanence, satisfactoriness and self that Buddha Dhamma specifically sets out to counter.

All these wrong views bring distress, sometimes great and agonising distress, because they cause people to attempt the literally impossible. How can such views be corrected? What should we do to correct our own wrong views?

Let me say right away that you cannot correct **all** wrong views. You cannot verify every opinion you have about the mundane world. You would be forever trying to do so. There is not enough time. It is not possible, nor is it necessary, to correct all mundane wrong views to come to the cessation of suffering, to the ending of suffering which is *nibbāna*. But you do need to get a few fundamental views straight. That is unavoidable.

The Teaching of the Buddha separates views into two kinds of particular relevance to the spiritual search: mundane and supramundane[1]. These are views relating to our ordinary world on the one hand, and those relating to the search for the ultimate on the other. There are five basic mundane views that are necessary to happy living here and now, as far as that is possible.

---

[1]   See notes on page 9.

The first mundane right view is that there is result of action. Every volitional action you do has some kind of resultant. Selfish actions lead to distress. Unselfish actions lead to pleasant results.

The second: There is a result of giving. If you are generous, if you give away some of your wealth and possessions, time and effort, then you get a very positive personal benefit from such open-handedness.

The third mundane right view is that parents are worthy of the greatest respect. In the original texts it is expressed in this way: 'There are mother and father.' This sounds very cryptic; of course there are mother and father – we would not be here otherwise. To hold this right view is to recognise that we owe a tremendous debt of gratitude to our parents for giving us the opportunity to be born human. Only in the human realm is it possible properly to approach the task of coming to the end of all suffering. We, human beings, are balanced roughly midway between the extremes of discomfort and pain that the hell states offer, and extreme pleasure, which is found in the heaven realms. This roughly equal balance of pain and pleasure enables us to recognise and apply ourselves to the middle path, the eightfold path. In this way, we can win the understanding of suffering necessary to escape from it.

The fourth mundane right view: There are spontaneously-arisen beings. There do exist beings in other realms, on other levels of existence, whom we cannot see with normal physical eyes. There are other realms, and those realms are places where we might take up residence having died from this plane of existence.

Lastly, there are teachers who know about these things from their own experience, and who can teach us about them. From them people can learn how to find out what is in their own best interests.

These five mundane right views provide a framework for living happily in the worlds as far as that is possible. While living happily in the world does not mean you can avoid all suffering and distress, acting with a view to results does ensure that life goes as smoothly as it can. If you act always with a selfish motive, you will experience pain and discomfort and disaster for the most part. If you act unselfishly, then so many blessings come your way, you wonder how it could possibly have happened.

There is another facet to right views: holding them, you develop a true understanding, a true 'feel for' self-responsibility. To accept these five right views is tacitly to accept that action and its results – painful or pleasant – are entirely our own responsibility. We may not blame anyone else for our good or ill fortune, for it is self-engineered. Where we are now, at this very moment – however we are placed, happy or unhappy – is a direct result of what we have done in the past. It does not matter what external circumstances may seem to have done to us, or for us, what we experience now is directly a result of our own past action. What we experience now is of course supported by the present conditions. It is, however, primarily a result of all we have done.

Mundane right view is a framework of ideas that allows the best possible existence in the world of *samsāra*. It does not eradicate suffering entirely. Within the world, that is impossible, for even good conditions are transient and therefore ultimately unsatisfactory. To consider how finally to eradicate all suffering, we need to look at supramundane right view.

Supramundane right view shows us a way out of the entire tangle. Supramundane right view comprises the last two of the four noble truths: there is a beyond (the third truth); there is a way to that beyond (the fourth). That way, the eightfold path, has eight 'steps': right view, right thought, right speech, right action, right livelihood, right effort, right mindfulness and right concentration.

It is easy to gloss over the many lists found in Buddhism, but it is well worth learning them by heart, for then you can reflect upon them in moments of leisure. Often you will find that after, or sometimes during, meditation, a particular word or phrase will come to mind, imbued with meaning which it did not have before. Had you not learned that word or phrase in the first place, that could not happen. Learning lists provides a very useful way of broadening the scope of meditation, quite apart from anything else.

The eightfold path is designed to eradicate the craving that leads to suffering. Craving is wanting things to be different. You could say that craving is wanting the impossible. It is wanting to find permanence where there can be no such thing. It is wanting to gain lasting happiness in this very world, here and now – which is manifestly impossible, for things constantly change.

With supramundane right view we expect to win freedom from suffering. We expect to find, use and work at a practical path leading to the beyond of the worlds, the beyond of suffering. We expect to win that freedom – but not in the known universe, for we recognise that the known universe is impermanent, unsatisfactory and non-self. Gaining freedom from wrong views (that things are permanent, satisfactory and can be owned) means to establish right views. We can do it only via the eightfold path, which is summarised in three sections: ethical conduct (*sīla*), meditation (*samādhi*) and wisdom (*paññā*).

Ethical conduct (*sīla*) is usually spoken of in connection with the five precepts. In their simplest form, these are injunctions to refrain from killing, stealing, unlawful sex, all kinds of wrong speech and intoxicating substances. More comprehensively, however, conduct needs to be 'right' by being based on the five points of mundane right view we looked at earlier. If it is not, you will suffer from guilt, you will suffer from worry, you will suffer from doubt. Guilt, worry and doubt completely prevent the mind from settling to the task of meditation. When you are distressed and agitated, sometimes you break out of the meditation feeling hot and bothered, not knowing why. You feel anxious, even when you are on your own. You feel worried about things, and are not sure why. If ethical conduct – *sīla* – is perfect, then those aggravations cannot occur, and the mind is relatively calm and stable, allowing one to practise another section of the eightfold path:

Meditation (*samādhi*): literally 'concentration' or, more properly, 'mindfulness and concentration'. Meditation is the skill of concentrating the attention on the rise and fall of all things, on the three marks[2] of all conditioned phenomena[3]: transience,

---

2   Three marks: aspects or signs (*lakkhana*) of objects. Just as hardness is a 'mark' of diamond and coldness an aspect of ice, so transience, inability to produce lasting satisfaction and dependence on multiple other factors are marks of all relative, or conditioned, things.

3   Conditioned phenomena: things and processes, mental and physical, which depend for their existence on other factors, conditions and things. The 'opposite' of the beyond, *nibbāna*. For example, suffering (*dukkha*) itself cannot exist without craving (*tanhā*), which in turn depends on ignorance (*avijjā*) for its existence.

unsatisfactoriness and non-self. It may include the deeply concentrated states known as the jhanas, the fixed meditations, but these are not absolutely necessary developments for supramundane insight to arise.

Wisdom (*paññā*): right view and right thought. Essentially, *paññā* is wisdom, and so you could say that it is 'right seeing'; it is seeing things as they are, specifically in terms of the three marks of all conditioned phenomena. Wisdom grows with application to the path, culminating in insight which leads to *nibbāna* – but no one starts his search without the wisdom that life is unsatisfactory.

How do you get to see things as they are? Yes, meditation, but how? There are two traditional routes, both of which are founded upon ethical discipline.

For the recluse who has much quiet time in secluded surroundings, the traditional route is to develop concentration and then the psychic powers. This, when successful, allows the individual to examine his own past lives, and to see how this action produced that result, repeatedly. In this way, the meditator can come to see action and result in operation over the span of many lifetimes.

The practice of deep concentration and the psychic powers is not necessary for the lay person – although it is unquestionably the best. Instead, you can gain a sufficient degree of the same understanding within ordinary life, by meditative observation. If you closely observe your actions and their results, you will find that you can verify the first three of the five mundane right views. For instance, if you closely observe generosity and the beneficial results that follow, you can prove for yourself that 'there is result of giving'. In this way, you get the same benefit as the recluse who goes back through his or her past lives.

So far, we have dealt only with the meditative development of mundane wisdom. When we come to consider the supramundane, there is only one route, whether for recluse or lay person. You have to use repeated direct observation to produce insight wisdom, or direct knowledge of things as they truly are. That direct knowledge, that insight, seeing the reality of things, destroys wrong views. The method is primarily to observe the mark of transience in all conditioned things. This meditation breaks down the wrong view of permanence and is one of the three gateways to freedom. The other two, unsatisfactoriness and non-self, are also used as the occasion demands.

We concentrate initially on perceiving impermanence, on seeing the fact that things rise and fall, they are transient. The resulting perception destroys the idea, the belief, the expectation that things are going to last. Coming to know for certain, by experience, that things do not last, there is no way you can then crave for things to continue. You **know** they do not. In this way craving is eradicated at its root.

☆ ☆ ☆

What of the person who has gone all the way through this training? How does he or she see the world? How do they appear to the world? How do they conduct themselves? What is the enlightened person really like? How many kinds of enlightened persons are there? Would you know one if you met one?

The enlightened person still has mundane views. He still has views about the way in which his world operates. It is not possible to live without them. He or she will have views about whether the Italian restaurant is a good or a bad one, for example. There are certain kinds of knowledge that are not changed in the least by enlightenment. The mundane world is infinite in its scope. No one, enlightened or otherwise, can know more than a fraction of all there is to know. The enlightened person will still be relatively uninformed about the mundane world in its vast complexity. If he was knowledgeable before, he will be knowledgeable afterwards. If he was as thick as two short planks before, he will be as thick as two short planks afterwards; still enlightened – but as thick as two short planks, nonetheless.

One's mundane knowledge does not change significantly with enlightenment, with freedom from suffering. Some enlightened people experience considerable difficulties in the world, owing to a shortage of mundane skills. If a meditator is socially inept before enlightenment, and does not undergo training to correct it, he will be just as socially inept afterwards. It all depends upon prior training. Someone who has followed the path of 'dry' insight will not deepen his or her understanding of the mundane world as much as someone with the skills to review many past lives. The benefits accruing to the practice of deep concentration and the psychic powers are very real. They include a richness and depth of understanding that can come from no other source.

Someone who has arrived at the cessation of suffering by following the paths of concentration and insight is 'freed both ways'. He or she will have a much greater understanding of *kamma* – of action and resultant – than someone who has walked the insight path only. He will have a much better understanding of how beings are born, and die, and are reborn. To that extent, he will live more at ease here and now; he will act more skilfully, having access to a wider range of mental skills. He will know the workings of the world in greater depth than someone who has not travelled that particular route.

Knowledge gained from the psychic powers is limited by the level of concentration a meditator can muster. With weak concentration, retrospection may be limited to just one or two past lives. Only Buddhas develop the psychic powers sufficiently to review an almost infinite length of past time, thereby to gain a deep knowledge of all aspects of the mundane world. They also develop the perfections (*parami*), which are various aspects of compassion. Such compassion leads Buddhas to work tirelessly, ceaselessly, for the good of all. It also ensures that they have the skills necessary to deliver their Teaching to the greatest effect.

The development of compassion is a most significant aspect of Buddhist training. It inculcates a set of disciplines that enable you to become very much more useful to your fellow human beings as you advance gradually along the path. There is a much greater chance that when you do eventually become enlightened, you can then lead others to the same cessation of suffering.

What of the enlightened being and supramundane views? How does he or she see the world? He sees nothing in mind or body as permanent, satisfactory or self. He cannot find anything at all, physical or mental, that is permanent. He cannot find anything at all, physical or mental, that is ultimately satisfactory. Nowhere can he find anything, physical or mental, which he can call a self, either in the mundane world or the beyond.

This being so, he does not crave for, nor cling to, any aspect of mind or body. He or she produces no suffering at all, for where there is no craving, where there is no clinging, there can be no suffering. In particular, he will be especially aware of transience, suffering or non-self, depending which mark was his vehicle for the escape from ignorance to enlightenment.

The goal of the Buddhist path, the complete eradication of

suffering in all its forms, is beyond the world as we know it. Exquisite attention to the transience of all relative phenomena is the one way to that goal. Such attention, when properly backed up by study, meditation and total commitment, eliminates wrong view by coming to see clearly things as they are. It is not an easy path – but it is an extremely effective one. I know of no better way to approach truth.

5

BEYOND GOOD AND EVIL

Many people have found themselves exercised over the problem of evil. What is it? How does it come into existence? How is it overcome? For some, the very existence of evil is a dilemma. How is it possible to reconcile evils such as starvation and warfare with the idea that the world is perfect as it is? How can one possibly say that things are all right when, manifestly, there are critical and possibly insuperable problems in the world today? How is it possible to suggest that we are all already perfect, that we are all *buddha* within[1], when the individual himself may feel sick to death of his life and may see everything through the darkest of clouds?

What is this thing called evil? How does it arise? Is it a real phenomenon or is it truly illusory, as some would claim?

The world, including all matter, mind and spirit, is perfect as it is. There is nothing excluded from this. The entire world **is** perfect and this fact is the basis for the Zen saying that *samsāra* and *nibbāna* are the same. The world is perfect; our ideas about the world are quite another matter. Any problems we have lie not in the world but in our views of the world and of ourselves. Of course, in the early stages of meditation practice, it is difficult to see that the world as we believe it to be is not at all the same thing as the world as it is. It is difficult to accept that we may not be seeing things clearly, even though we have come to meditation to learn to eradicate blindness.

In *nibbāna* there is no strife, no conflict and no war. At the highest level there is only harmony, unity and non-separation. All is truly one or, more accurately, not two. Reality is all of a

---

[1] *Buddha* within: some say that all beings have the 'buddha-nature' within, that we are in one sense already enlightened, or perfected, though we do not know it. Our task is therefore to expand our awareness to discover that this is the case.

piece, with no gaps or breaks, with no exclusions, with no division anywhere. There is no separation, no separate individual, no separate self, no this or that, no good or bad, no high or low. All opposites are transcended. At this rarefied level evil does not and cannot exist; there is no such thing. Evil belongs strictly to the relative universe. It does not exist at all in the highest, in *nibbāna*. Evil is something based entirely on misunderstandings and partial views of life. It can exist only when there is an ignorance of the truly indivisible nature of reality. At the highest level there is no separation between me and you. We are indivisibly united. We have never been apart.

The path of learning is to come to accept that there is no separation between beings, for beings do not actually exist as separate and discrete entities. It is to come to see that all ways of separation and division are evil (or negative) and all ways of love and concord are good (or positive). Having seen the truth of good and evil, then we know that estrangement from reality (some would say, from God) results in experience that is in its very nature suffering. This applies most obviously at the mundane level of evil, where others are seen as separate and inferior, but also applies at the mundane level of good, for this too marks an estrangement at the very least into separate beings.

Thus the final answer is to transcend both good and evil; to see that both good and evil do not (really) exist. From the highest point of view there is no good and there is no evil; there is only reality that is love. Love, in this sense, is the total absence of separation and dualistic experience. It is utter fulfilment, although there is nothing to be fulfilled and no fulfilment either.

'Evil' is any action or belief that results in a sense of isolation and separation from the true and the real. Based entirely on wrong views of oneself and of the universe, it operates at several distinct levels, as we shall see. There is a spectrum of evil that ranges from the most gross behaviour all the way through to things that normally we might consider quite acceptable.

Think of the things you personally find painful, the things that try you sorely. Consider the trials of anger and frustration, of strife and conflict with a partner, family or friends. Consider the arid facts of loneliness and isolation. Think of the times when you have felt low; when your self-esteem was shrivelled and warped. Think of the times when you have been depressed, sad or unhappy.

What is common to all these conditions? What is the hallmark of such states? Track it down. See it for what it is. It's the sense of separation from all that you hold good and true, from all that you consider most worthwhile in life. It does not matter whether your assessment of the situation is accurate – indeed it cannot be, for otherwise you could not suffer the way you do. What does matter is the sense of separateness that your outlook causes. That separation is what people call evil.

You can feel yourself to be separated from the world around you in many different ways. You may be isolated socially, by having few if any friends, by working unsocial hours, by keeping yourself to yourself all the time. If you transgress the laws of the land, you may be physically isolated from society for a time, by being sent to prison. If you commit serious crimes against your fellows, in some places today you would be isolated 'permanently' from the whole human race: you would be executed. Short of death or torture, one of the worst punishments that can be visited on prisoners the world over is that of isolation, of solitary confinement. All such separation is a desperate trial if you believe that you are the physical body, as 99 percent of people do, and you desire greatly all the things of the body.

Although loneliness is a great problem for some, most people avoid these obvious forms of separation and instead suffer from others, no less real, but perhaps less obvious at first glance.

One of the most common forms of isolationist, evil behaviour is criticism. This can show itself in various ways, from the nagging husband or wife, to the more subtle but devastating emotional pressures brought to bear in many a relationship. The relationship does not even need to be particularly close. It may be between employer and employee, between salesman and prospective victim. The attempt at domination through emotional pressure is the projection of an overwhelming sense of disapproval or even contempt for the person who will not do what you want. It is a form of blackmail, for it says, 'I will isolate you if you do not comply.' The person on the receiving end is left in no doubt as to his or her options. Often, they fear the separation and isolation so much that they end up doing something quite out of character, usually to their subsequent regret.

Moody people tend to use emotional blackmail to get what

they want. They are so attached to feelings that they will use any emotional ploy to try to bring the world to heel.

Emotional separation can be traumatic. Anyone who has experienced the rigours of a divorce knows well the pain and anguish of emotional separation and knows too that it takes a long time to recover from. Those who have observed the process carefully also know that the intense suffering is not the other person's fault. They know that the suffering is due to the resentment, hatred and confusion in their own minds. It is these things that are the evil, for it is thoughts based on resentment and hatred, or on attachment and the refusal to accept the changing pattern of life, that produce the sense of isolation.

There can be a similar problem with bereavement. Attachment to the ways things were – or to the idea of how they might have been – often leads to a whole range of emotional disturbances for those left behind. Anger and resentment directed at the deceased for being so inconsiderate as to die, now, are commonly part of the grieving process. Self-pity, depression and a sense of the futility of life are commonplace. There can be an almost overwhelming sense of isolation and loneliness and life can seem very daunting in prospect.

While some of these emotional states are probably unavoidable when someone close to you dies, it is unquestionably the case that protracted grief is only possible if the bereaved attempts always to cling on to the deceased. It needs the attachment, or clinging, to produce the distress.

You can experience an intellectual separation when you find that your ideas are out of step with those around you. You are not 'on the same wavelength'. You cannot communicate your deeper musings to the others with whom you live or work. This sense of separation and isolation can be just as trying as any of the others. It is just as real and just as traumatic. Again, the problem is not in the difference in thinking patterns as such. The frustration is due to desiring desperately to communicate and yet not being able to succeed. It is the desire, the attachment to the idea of communication, which is the 'evil'.

Finally there is what we might call spiritual separation. This can be the 'dark night of the soul' when all seems futile and yet there is at the same time a feeling that, somewhere, there is an answer. Hating the dark, desiring the light and having for the time being lost one's way, there is a terrible sense of isolation, of separateness, which is frightening to experience. At a lower level, this kind of separation is also engendered by pride and conceit. If you are 'puffed up', if you over-estimate your own worth in any field, material, emotional or spiritual, then you will find that you suffer terribly from a feeling of isolation and separation. You will 'feel bad' about it and you will feel somehow 'out of touch' with your universe.

It is always the views and attitudes of mind that are the evil conditions, not the circumstances themselves. The conditions certainly are *dukkha*, suffering, but this is an inevitable outcome of the evil actions of hatred and attachment, arising from self-view and a distorted view of the universe. It is the views that are wrong, not the circumstances.

☆ ☆ ☆

Every once in a long, long while, a great man or woman discovers a way to overcome the evil that exists in the world. They discover a way through to the truth of things as they are. The teaching we are committed to here is the Teaching of the Buddha, a man born over 2,500 years ago. The way he left for us is so strong and powerful that it has survived intact through twenty-five centuries; it is as fresh and as relevant today as ever it was. Today, just as then, it is possible to come to the fullest flower of that Teaching if only you exert yourself diligently and faithfully enough.

There is a short verse in the *Dhammapada* that sums up the Buddha's entire Teaching. 'Cease to do evil, learn to do good, purify the mind – this is the Teaching of the Buddhas.' [*Dhammapada 183*].

'Good' is any action or idea that results in harmony and concord. It is that which reduces the sense of separateness and isolation from reality that so many people experience. By nature, good is opposed to evil. Just as there is a spectrum of evil so too is there a spectrum of good. Good action and thought can operate at the levels of body, emotion, intellect and spirit. Evil is counteracted by good. The two are always fighting for balance in the world. Good exists only in relation to evil. Evil exists only in relation to good.

Good reduces the sense of separation in many ways. We can become good at the physical level, by taking on the burden of ethical behaviour as outlined in the five precepts. This reduces antisocial tendencies and thereby increases the harmony and concord within a group of people.

An extension of this principle, which is very effective for certain character types, is to devote themselves to the service of others. You can see this at its purest in the lives of those monastics who follow the way of devotion. Such people care little or nothing for themselves. They are committed to serving others with everything they possess. For them, always the other person is the more important. It is a wonderful way of reducing pride, conceit, selfishness and all negative qualities. It promotes concord and undercuts evil as almost nothing else can.

The ideal of service can be followed without the necessity of becoming a monk or a nun. You can apply it in your day-to-day dealings with those close to you at home and at work. All it takes is the recollection that harmony and concord are a step closer to the highest than are states such as anger, criticism, selfishness and contempt. This could be called 'loving-kindness (*mettā*) in action', for it is a fundamental principle of loving-kindness to wish the other person well in whatever they do.

Following such a course of action, you will find that many difficulties are alleviated as if by magic. Marital conflict diminishes. Power struggles at work fade away. The sense of loneliness and isolation one might have felt before is replaced by a sense of being once again a part of life. The more you give, the more you extend consideration and compassion to others, the more you grow in communion with your world and the more your loneliness is eased.

To help the sick, the needy and the downtrodden is another way of offering service. You have to be very careful, though, for it is all too easy to start to feel superior when helping those worse off than yourself. If that were to happen, then the very object of the exercise would have been defeated.

I read the other day of a singer; in the doldrums and having a really bad time, she felt totally isolated from her surroundings and was extremely unhappy. In the depths of her misery she remembered something she had heard a long while before. She remembered hearing someone say that you have to give to get back. So she bought a dog. She bought a dog upon which she could lavish affection without fear of reprisals and, from that time, her life began to change. Gradually she turned herself around. The love and care offered to another living being reduced the selfishness in her own character and put her back in touch with the world. It reduced her sense of isolation and she again became a fully-functioning member of the community. This is the power of love and service.

At a more rarefied level you can learn to go beyond evil by developing the practice of concentration. Using the power of right concentration, it is possible completely to suppress all evil states of mind and to experience only the good. Such experience dramatically reduces the sense of separation and isolation at the time. However, the state cannot last and when the meditation practice wears off, as it is bound to do, the 'normal world' can seem uglier than it did before.

Good action, good behaviour, is not the final answer to all man's problems. How could it be? Good is merely a temporary stage on the path of evolution. It still has strong traces of separateness in it. It is still 'me against the world', even if in a vastly more subtle form than that deriving from aggression, hatred and attachment. The individual who pours his heart into helping others, in nearly all cases, is not doing it only for them. He or she is doing it for personal profit and satisfaction. There is very much present the idea of 'separate beings' and consequently there is present as well a definite state of suffering. If there is a sense of separateness, even at the level of completely altruistic behaviour, there is also *dukkha*: pain, suffering and dissatisfaction.

Wherever there is the intention to eradicate suffering, either your own or that of others, there is a subtle disturbance of the mind. To aim at anything is to experience further separation. Craving to overcome distress creates its own problem. Hatred of evil and negativity produces an imbalance in the mind and resultant suffering. It is necessary to come to accept the fact of evil. It is necessary to cease to hate even this.

Equanimity is the key. See all things with the eye of equanimity. Learn to be content with pain or pleasure, success or failure, progress or regress. Put aside ambition and personal bias. Learn to be even-minded.

One way to control the (natural) problems of partiality and ambition is to take exquisite pains to be 'mindful and self-possessed'. The meditator takes care always to maintain the balance of mind between the extremes of elation and depression. When successful, he will be far less affected by 'good' and 'evil' and, to that extent, nearer to reality (and further away from suffering).

In your meditation practice it is essential to cease to react negatively against the facets of your character that you judge to be negative. There needs to be the development of compassion for one's own negativity. There needs to be an understanding tolerance of the negative within you, so that you may lay to rest the vicious and pernicious activities of mind that have for so long prevented you seeing the true face of the world. You cannot become enlightened if you hate yourself. You cannot become enlightened if you love yourself in a conceited and prideful way. You have to transcend this aspect of personal criticism and judgement in favour of a simple, unbiased acknowledgement of what is present, whether 'good' or 'bad'.

This is to become truly 'yourself', to stop trying always to adjust circumstances to your own likes and dislikes, to stop always moaning or exulting about your own lot in life, to accept all there is gracefully. To accept all there is means just that. You have to accept yourself, 'warts and all'. You have to accept the bad things and the good things. You have ultimately to accept that whatever there is in your character is not evil in itself – it is your reaction to it that is the problem. You are attached to craving, you are attached to hatred, you are attached to confusion. It is this attachment that is the problem. Get rid of it by replacing it with equanimity and you will experience a sense of freedom that is truly remarkable. It is a true harbinger of the end of separation.

As equanimity develops, the capacity to observe the arising and passing away of all things grows. You begin to see more clearly one or another of the three marks of all conditioned phenomena.

You may become more aware that things really are transient: they change all the time and with such rapidity that it is questionable whether they can accurately be said to exist at all. Or perhaps it is the mark of *dukkha*, suffering, that becomes more apparent. In this case you will come to see by direct experience that there is nothing that is ultimately satisfactory: all things, no matter how 'good' or how exalted, are ultimately unable to satisfy you. They will never provide a support for true happiness.

If you become attuned to the mark of *anattā*, non-self, you will see that all things are interrelated and that there is no way in which anything can really be separated from anything else. All things are intertwined so inextricably that it is not possible to say that anything exists independently of anything else. This being so, there is no separate self and there is no thing that could possibly be owned even if there were: there is no 'me' and no 'mine'. The very concept of ownership, whether of body or of anything else, is seen to be a pure myth.

Knowledge arises that there is no final solution in good, for it is as transient as is evil in the long term. In this sense they are the same, good and evil, for they are both relative and not the final answer that man seeks.

It becomes obvious that it is necessary to transcend even the subtle sense of separation that is engendered by being and doing good. Forget about being a person who is supposed to behave in a certain way. Be content with whatever arises and come to know that all sense of separation is illusion. 'Things' are in fact so utterly transient that they can truly be said not to exist. And yet that is not to say that there is nothing there. There is **this**. There is **reality**. There is non-division, non-separation. This is truly 'to be in touch' with everything. There is no longer any isolation or loneliness. The paradox has been resolved.

With freedom from the relative comes the recognition that there are two levels to the mind. There is the relative and mundane level and there is the real level: the level of *nibbāna*, or reality. At the relative level we can act **as if** men, mountains and trees actually exist, although we know that these are convenient and arbitrary fictions. We understand, now, that the labels we put on things are not accurate. All they provide is a convenient shorthand way of referring to something. They do not and cannot fix the reality, or non-reality, of anything. They are just made-up, convenient terms that we can use to communicate, rather sketchily, with others. At the other level of the mind there is all the time a direct knowledge of the deeper truth that all is perfect as it is and that there is no separation of any 'one' from any 'thing': all is truly perfect as it is.

The absence of separation means just what it says: there is no longer any sense of isolation from any aspect of the universe, seen or unseen. There comes to be a feeling of kinship with all life, whether animal or vegetable, mineral or mental. Nothing is excluded from the smallest to the largest, from the most obviously visible to the invisible.

There is no more isolation from human beings, animals, trees, plants, devas, gods, demons, the rich, the poor, the downtrodden and all those many, many others. There is no longer any separation from the earth on which we live, for even rocks and metals are alive at their own level, as are things made from the earth and its constituents.

Some call this 'union' but, in truth, there is no thing to be joined to any other thing, for there never was any separation in the first place. It was simply the fact that our **ideas** about life, the universe and everything were sadly askew and that we acted in a crazy fashion based on wrong information. Having come by experience to know that the information was false, having corrected our wrong views about things, now there is the bliss of 'coming home' to the place we have never left.

At this point we realise that, in one sense, our journey was never necessary, for there has never been anywhere to go and there has never been anywhere to leave. All is perfect as it is and it has never been any different from perfect. Truly we have achieved nothing by enlightenment. There is simply the shedding of all views about self and its place in the universe. With that shedding of view and opinion, what is always there is discovered, hidden like a jewel in a dung-heap.

The total freedom and bliss of enlightenment are not far, far away. Freedom is nearer to you than the air you breathe, nearer than the blood in your veins, nearer even than the thoughts you think. True freedom can never be lost; it can only be covered over temporarily by a mist of views. Blow away the mist. Go beyond thoughts of good and evil and there you find the Buddha Within, eternally present and ever available.

6

STARTING TO MEDITATE

The Buddha summarised his entire Teaching in four noble truths. A clear understanding of these is both the start and the end of the Buddhist way to freedom. He said:

There exists suffering.
There exists a cause of suffering.
There exists the complete eradication of suffering.
There exists a way leading to the complete eradication of suffering.

Following the Buddha's Teaching is often spoken of as taking refuge in the Buddha, taking refuge in the Dhamma, his Teaching, and taking refuge in the Sangha, the body of people who practise that Teaching. The Sangha is usually thought of as an order of monks and nuns, but in a wider sense includes all who are intent upon the path, ordained or lay. Whether or not one formally goes for refuge, taking up the practice of the Buddha's Teaching is just that – going for refuge in the Buddha, the Dhamma and the Sangha.

The Buddha carefully defined a systematic path by which individuals could attain enlightenment. This eightfold path, when followed with dedication, enables men and women of any age and any culture to become aware of things they had never known before. It allows the gradual extension of the boundaries of perception until the last veil hiding the unknown is stripped away. All eight 'steps' interlock, but it is easier to consider them separately or in three sections.

Wisdom (*paññā*):   Right view
                      Right thought

Behaviour (*sīla*):	Right speech
	Right action
	Right livelihood
Meditation (*samādhi*):	Right effort
	Right mindfulness
	Right concentration

Wisdom is both the start and the end of the path: one needs at least a sketchy awareness of the all-pervasiveness of suffering to see the need to follow a way to freedom; at the end of the path there is full understanding of the eradication of suffering. In practical terms, however, the first element of the path that concerns those new to the Teaching is behaviour (*sīla*), discipline, personal conduct.

The very first element in the training is to try to live by a number of rules of behaviour. For the lay person there are five: the five precepts. The novice is bound by ten precepts, and there are **many** more rules of training for monks and nuns. These rules are designed to render personal behaviour harmless to others and to oneself, thus maximising one's chances of developing the meditative mind. They are not in any sense commandments. As rules of **training**, they take due account of human fallibility. If he breaks one, a lay person reaffirms his commitment to the precepts and resolves to do better in future.

The rules of conduct are essentially a means of self-training. How do they work? Take, perhaps, a very simple case: refraining from stealing. To refrain from stealing is to limit one's own selfish desires, to put a check on them, to restrain oneself from actions that otherwise one might take. To the extent that such restraint is successful, personal behaviour is already less selfish than before.

The extended form of that rule is 'to refrain from taking that which is not given'. This is much more subtle.

Say you are living in a rooming-house where you share the kitchen. Late for work, you go to the fridge only to find you have run out of milk. But there are three pints in the rack, each belonging to a different person. You think, 'I'm sure Gerry won't mind ...' And you 'borrow' some of his milk. What happens? Gerry **does** mind and friction develops where there was none before. The incident turns quite nasty and you have lost a friend

– all because you took something that was not given. It was very easy to do. Borrowing the milk seemed harmless at the time and you were quite certain that Gerry would not mind (although **you** would have been upset had someone used yours). Because of selfish desire, you introduced disharmony into what might otherwise have continued to be a harmonious environment.

The five precepts cover the more obvious occasions for misbehaviour. Those for lay people are:

I undertake the rule of training to refrain from ...

... killing or harming living creatures.
... taking that which is not given.
... wrongful sexual conduct.
... lying, slander, gossip and all forms of wrong speech.
... strong drink and intoxicating substances.

The objective of these rules of behaviour is self-training by restraint; we train ourselves to refrain from treading on other people's toes. If we can limit our own selfish desires, our selfish cravings, by following the precepts in their extended forms, life gets a great deal more comfortable and satisfying, and we begin to see the world around us more clearly.

Keeping the precepts in this way, we may attain 'the perfection of mere morality' in the course of training. We can get to the point where personal conduct is perfect – perfect, that is, in being as unselfish as possible within worldly conditions. We never put a foot wrong; we never break a rule either in its obvious or in its extended form. Whether we are talking about lay people, or monks and nuns, it is possible to get to the point where discipline cannot be improved further.

There is a particular point to such restraint: it quietens the mind and removes some major obstacles to progress on the spiritual path. As we succeed in following the rules of conduct, fear and guilt diminish. If conduct is perfect, fear – of being found out, of the future, of upsetting people – completely disappears. Guilt no longer arises because you know for certain you have not done anything for which you need feel guilty. You can look anyone in the eye, knowing that your personal conduct is beyond reproach. Do you still suffer from fear and guilt? If the question makes you uneasy, then there is some work still to do.

Absence of guilt and fear – ease of living to that extent – is the culmination, the peak of perfection of *sīla*, personal conduct, and provides the perfect platform from which to launch the meditative journey. There is not much more you can do by restraint of bodily action alone. Trying further to refine your physical behaviour moment by moment will not bring you any nearer to understanding and insight. It is, however, possible to safeguard your endeavour towards enlightenment by making sure that your lifestyle and livelihood are compatible with your overall aim. It is senseless to practise impeccable personal restraint if your worldly ambitions are at odds with your spiritual objectives.

Right livelihood at its most conspicuous level is abstaining from activities that have goals opposed to the search for the end of suffering. These include such things as trading in weapons, in living beings, in intoxicants and in poisons for the purpose of killing living beings. Right livelihood also is to abstain from occupations like slaughtering, fishing and soldiering, as well as to refrain from deceit, treachery, soothsaying, fraud, usury and other enterprises that place personal profit ahead of others' welfare.

There is a subtle aspect of right livelihood that can be a trap for the unwary. This is not so much what you do as the way in which you do it. For instance, working excessively hard to change yourself, to become something different and better, you set into motion 'becoming' (*bhava*), the whole process of birth, growth, decay, death and suffering. Excessive ambition directed towards mundane objectives always carries a high price-tag in increased distress.

Some maintain that zealously working towards the eradication of suffering produces similar problems and that it is necessary to put aside even the ambition to become enlightened. This is not quite the case. While unwise application and excessive effort can hinder progress, nothing at all will be accomplished without serious efforts towards enlightenment.

The quest for truth and understanding has to be pursued with the utmost diligence and care if success is to be won. Certainly, the craving for enlightenment brings distress, but it also brings direction. You need to direct your efforts towards understanding, towards escape from the thrall of ignorance and craving, for any progress to be made.

Your objective as a meditator is to organise your life so that you can best pay attention to the three marks of all conditioned phenomena. All your efforts then are geared towards living in a way that encourages awareness to grow. Your lifestyle will support your meditative efforts so that understanding of the three marks and understanding of conditioning increase steadily. In time this leads to the development of insight that will break the fetters binding you to the wheel of suffering.

None of this is 'useful' in the way that working towards a mundane goal such as accountancy or bricklaying is useful. It does not have any immediately applicable single purpose in the world. But the training, if followed through, enhances anything to which you choose to turn your attention.

To go further than 'the perfection of mere morality', we have to look at another section of the eightfold path – *samādhi*, concentration or meditation. The restraint of personal bad conduct is absolutely necessary but while it undeniably reduces personal distress, it cannot eliminate suffering altogether. Something else is needed. Meditation is the next step. We find that having learned something of restraint from keeping the precepts and rejecting excessive self-profit, we have now to refine it greatly. Meditation demands greater and more subtle restraint.

☆ ☆ ☆

Meditation, pretty well of whatever kind, is designed to develop the two faculties of mindfulness and concentration. This development needs an object to focus on, yet the object must be something that does not cause us to get self-absorbed in the wrong way. There are many possible choices: the books list 40 different objects, though not all are suitable for all character types. Experience shows that the meditation object that suits just about everyone is the feeling of breathing, either at the nose-tip or as the sensation of the rise and fall of the abdomen which takes place with each in- and out-breath.

Curiously, many people when they first start meditation cannot easily perceive the feeling of rising and falling in the abdominal area. Or if they can when they start it soon goes, and they find they are in difficulties: they cannot find anything to focus on. In consequence, the first part of the meditative exercise consists of learning how properly to contact the feeling in the abdomen (or the nose-tip, if that is how you have been taught). You learn how to isolate the feeling, to know what you are looking at and to get a precise feel for (pun absolutely intended) what is going on.

With practice, you will find that it is possible to develop a clear perception of the feeling of rise and fall as it occurs in the abdomen. The problem, though, is that your attention continually gets dragged off on to other things, distractions of one sort or another: sounds, other feelings, thoughts – you name it. The difficulty then is learning how to deal with this kind of disturbance.

Many people try to force their way through, and as a result get particularly tense and uncomfortable. With persistence in this enthusiastic but unwise approach, they often experience headaches and great physical discomfort. Typical complaints are of extreme muscle pains in the shoulders and back, a painfully stiff neck, nausea and twitching limbs or, in women of a certain age, hot flushes. Such discomfort is avoidable. The trick is simply to acknowledge the different distractions by name, recognising that they are an integral part of the practice, and gently – and I do mean gently – return the attention to the feeling of rise and fall in the abdomen. Continuing to practise in this way, you find that after a time the mind simply loses interest in the distractions and focuses more acutely on the feeling of rise and fall.

At that point you can introduce the next step, which is mentally to follow the feeling of rise and fall as though you were stalking an animal. You stalk it, you follow that feeling, from the bottom of the fall right through to the top of the rise. As it turns over, you follow it down again, trying never to let it out of your mental sight. If you can manage it, you will find that your concentration improves dramatically. But, of course, it works only if mindfulness is present as well as concentration. If mindfulness is not strong enough, you will find you tend to drift off into daydream and get sleepy. If on the other hand you try too hard, you will get tense and agitated again. It is 'gently, gently catchee monkey' the whole time.

As you learn the correct balance of effort and observation, as mindfulness grows, as concentration grows, you will find that everything you observe comes more sharply into focus. You can see more clearly just what is going on. That clarity of vision, that accuracy of perception, becomes a very sound basis for insight because it becomes obvious **from direct experience** that things do not last; they come and go. You watch the mark of *anicca*, transience, with ever-increasing clarity. Some say that things change but they do not: they dissolve, they die. The Buddhist maxim 'Any change in a thing is a change of thing' begins to make sense; you learn that transience is not change but mortality.

Attention should be cultivated not just in the periods of seated meditation, but in everything you do, internally and externally. Adherence to the rules of training will have started to focus the attention on the work-a-day world. Deliberate efforts to attend to every action help greatly to develop the capacity to observe things as they are. There are meditation exercises, the four foundations of mindfulness, designed specifically to aid the meditator in developing systematic attention. One of these, mindfulness of body, we will be looking at in some detail later.

In the end you find that the only way properly to pay attention is to observe whatever is present, always with a view to its transience. Through the working day, this could be listening to a lecture, paint-stripping, eating a meal, digging in the garden or sorting out an insurance claim. In seated meditation, you pay attention to individual sensations, sounds and other sensory happenings, or to boredom, confusion, tiredness, happiness and all other states. You discover that you have to deal with anything and everything in exactly the same way: quietly, mindfully, without craving, without hatred; ideally with gladness in the mind, and fully accepting of what is there. With such supreme balance in your personal life, you have the perfect basis for developing further.

It is a gentle, gradual development. You cannot do it all in one go; you have to work up to it. Success rests not only on the correct balance of effort and concentration, but also on the development of right mindfulness. It is this factor that seems very difficult for people at first to understand. It is common for new meditators to believe strongly that any problem can be overcome by effort and concentration alone, and for them entirely to miss the significance of setting up mindfulness. This has to be remedied if progress is to be made.

☆ ☆ ☆

From time to time, it is worth reflecting on what we are trying to do when we meditate. You could say – very loosely – that we are trying to make the unconscious conscious. What do you suppose that means?

In the mind, there are all kinds of activities going on which people choose to ignore. These activities are not unconscious, as some argue, for they arise, **are noticed momentarily** and are then ignored. They are found so unappealing that the mind rushes away immediately on to something else. Some people cannot admit that they have hatred in the mind, so they ignore it. Some ignore craving. Most of us try to ignore the perception that something is very fleeting, that it is transient. We then hide that fact and desperately try to convince ourselves, through a fantasy, that the object is lasting, that it is wonderful and that it is what we always wanted.

There is a brief moment when the true state of affairs is apparent. Immediately after that, the mind settles quickly into its habitual groove and all manner of inefficiency arises. We perform actions associated with ignorance, craving and hatred – and their countless offspring.

As anything has to be noticed in the first place before it can be ignored, it should be possible to see the true nature of experience simply by being more aware. And so it is. If you are alert enough, you can see the moment of reality that occurs before the mind obscures it by ignorance, craving, hatred, the hindrances and all the other mental poisons. It is not that you have particularly to do anything. You have instead to become more aware of what is already going on. You could say, loosely and inaccurately, that you have to make the unconscious conscious.

Such moments of reality might include things that, conventionally speaking, you would prefer not to admit to yourself. Most people think that they could not happily admit to negative tendencies like covetousness, jealousy or hatred. For some people, though, positive tendencies are a problem.

One male meditator had a very gentle nature; he was compassionate and loving. He liked to think of himself as rough and tough, though, and found it very difficult to admit to his softer side, even when he had seen it in meditation. It was quite contrary to the image of himself he wished to cultivate. It is not only the negative things that we hide from ourselves but sometimes the positive things as well.

Negative or positive, the key is still the same. It is learning to be more attentive to what is going on, without trying to change it. If you try to change it, you are constantly caught up in the battle of cravings and hatreds. You lack, at that time, the objectivity clearly to observe just what is taking place.

Once you know what is going on, then – perhaps – you can make adjustments if you need to. The pre-eminent faculty to develop is mindfulness.

7

MINDFULNESS OF BODY

As a child, I learned that there was a pot of gold at the end of the rainbow. You had only to dig where the rainbow came to earth to find the pot containing uncountable riches. This idea fired my imagination and I spent many days chasing rainbows whenever they appeared. I discovered, of course, that you could never, ever get to the end. You move, and the end of the rainbow moves – continually receding as you advance. The pot of gold, real or imaginary, is forever impossible to find.

We grow out of searching for literal pots of gold at the ends of literal rainbows, but we usually substitute other goals, other ways to find happiness, often just as impossible to achieve. Some pin their hopes on finding the perfect relationship. Some believe that the answer to unhappiness lies in wealth and power. Others put more store by recognition, believing that to be famous is a sure way to ease the burden of distress and that it will make up for any hardship. Yet others believe that the answer to suffering lies in faith and prayer, and take up the religious life. Cutting themselves off from the world, they undertake a life of privation and discipline, the better to earn forgiveness for their sins. A few choose wisdom in place of forgiveness – and turn, instead, to a way where the accent is on discovering for oneself how to overcome suffering.

The Buddha described his Teaching as 'come and see' (*ehi passiko*), a way to test and prove for oneself. He discovered that mind is intrinsically pure and free from suffering. It is the defilements themselves that are the problem. Suffering is a kind of overlay, a covering, a stain in mind-stuff that is of itself pure and perfect.

The Buddha taught that suffering arises from a cause: craving, itself arising from ignorance of the true facts of life. We strain and strive to attain those things that are literally impossible – like trying to find the pot of gold at the end of the rainbow. When we come to see this for ourselves – that certain things can never, ever be brought into existence – then the craving for them stops as if it had never been. With the ending of craving, no suffering can arise; the job is done.

It is easy to summarise, but trying to put it into practice is considerably more difficult. We need to develop certain skills before we can properly start on the journey to freedom. The first of these skills is mindfulness. It is the cornerstone of the Buddha's entire practical training; without it, it is not possible to realise freedom from suffering.

So what is mindfulness? Mindfulness is the opposite of ignorance. Ignorance is a deliberate turning away from what is present; mindfulness is a deliberate movement of mind towards what is present. It is awareness and clear comprehension of whatever aspect of mind and body is present in the moment.

Note that to be mindful is not to be aware of everything at once, but only that small slice of experience that is occurring right now. The Buddha analysed the human being into four areas of experience: body, feeling, states of mind and mental objects. Breaking it down in this way makes it easier for meditators to apply themselves to the task of setting up mindfulness – and thus to acquire its benefits.

So what is mindfulness not? Mindfulness is not 'being aware of yourself being aware of', say, walking. As an analogy, imagine a skilled craftsman practising his art. Do you suppose he is constantly saying to himself, 'Now I am being a carpenter' (or 'a programmer', 'a musician', 'a brain surgeon')? Of course not. He knows exactly what he is doing (he is 'mindful and self-possessed'), but there is no thought of self or what pertains to self. There is only clear awareness of the object or activity, whatever it may be. Mindfulness is definitely not self-conscious awareness.

What are the benefits of mindfulness? The benefits of the correct practice of mindfulness are experiential knowledge of mind and body and the wisdom that will then arise. But we can be more specific. Practising mindfulness leads to the acquisition of the 'seven factors of enlightenment' (*bojjhanga*), sometimes called the seven limbs of awakening. They are:

Mindfulness itself (*sati*) – unself-conscious alertness.

Investigation of Dhamma (*dhamma-vicaya*) – probing into mind and body to discover the reality behind appearances.

Energy (*viriya*) – correct expenditure of effort.

Rapture (*pīti*) – captivating and pleasurable interest in the object under investigation.

Tranquillity (*passaddhi*) – great peacefulness of body and mind, being completely settled in the task of meditation.

Concentration (*samādhi*) – withdrawal from the superficial, essentially; absence of distraction, and a tight focus on specific detail. And lastly:

Equanimity (*upekkhā*) – mental balance, complete absence of the passionate response to events, even-mindedness.

These seven factors of enlightenment lead to the acquisition of wisdom, notably the capacity to destroy the roots of ignorance, craving and hatred on which all suffering is based. For instance, with investigation into Dhamma, tranquillity and concentration, the faculties sharpen to allow full perception of transience. Development of the seven factors of enlightenment leads to a clear perception of things arising and passing away, transience, as well as the other two marks of all conditioned phenomena.

The development of mindfulness therefore leads to the practice of *vipassanā*, insight meditation, which in turn leads to the cessation of suffering. The Buddha described this as 'the one way', which some people see as a dogmatic statement. But it is the one way; you could say mindfulness is the only way. It is of course present in other formal religious paths but as far as I know only Buddha Dhamma, the Teaching of the Buddha, sets out in detail exactly how to develop every aspect of it.

How do you develop mindfulness? You develop it by setting up the four foundations of mindfulness: mindfulness of body, feeling, states of mind and mental objects. At first, meditators often find the three mental foundations too subtle to distinguish easily, but mindfulness of body provides the perfect starting-point. As you get better at perceiving mindfully all aspects of body, the other foundations become clear to you without specific effort. In proportion as body becomes clear, so too do feeling, states of mind and mental objects – more of which later.

To set up mindfulness of body is simply a matter of correct

practice. Anyone can do it, but it is necessary to be systematic. The Buddha offered several suggestions to his recluses. For example, he suggested setting up mindfulness of body by concentrating on the feeling of the in-and-out breath at the nose-tip, much as we do on the rise and fall of the abdomen. He suggested paying attention to changes of posture. There are only four, essentially: standing, sitting, lying down and walking. Part of the practice is to know in which posture the body is at any time, and to acknowledge and recognise the change from one posture to another.

Other aspects of body that form a basis for the development of mindfulness are things like bending and stretching, and setting out and returning. Typically, a monk in the Buddha's day would practise mindfulness on his alms-round. He would be mindful when setting out, while walking, while receiving food, while returning to base and while consuming the meal he had been given. Many people can be mindful of setting out, but getting back again, returning, is often quite a different matter.

Mindfulness of body can be broken down further. One can look at the body in terms of elements. Traditionally these are earth, air, fire and water. Some today dismiss this way of looking at materiality as superstition, but these terms represent the fundamental basis of all our experience of matter. For instance, earth represents hardness and softness, or pressure, to the tactile sense, and extension in space, as shape or colour, to the eye. Fire represents the awareness of temperature, both hot and cold; and air the sense of motion and movement. Water represents the cohesive force that binds the other three elements and, as such, is something that can only be inferred rather than directly experienced. Systematic and detailed attention to the direct experience of materiality, body, as the four elements is a powerful practice for setting up mindfulness.

The Buddha once asked a group of monks what methods they used to set up their practice. One monk said that he tried to be mindful going for alms and coming back again. Another said he tried to be mindful right the way through eating the meal he had been given on the alms-round. Another monk indicated that he preferred to be mindful while eating just one mouthful of food – and then the next mouthful, and the next. Yet another monk said he preferred to be mindful simply for one in-breath, and one out-breath, and then the next, and the next. Having heard the replies, the Buddha remarked that only the last two were practising the setting up of mindfulness in the proper manner. They were breaking their practice down into small units – a mouthful, an in-breath – and constantly repeating the exercise of paying attention with as much clarity as they could muster.

Another method of developing mindfulness of body is based on the 'thirty-two parts of the body', where the physical body is divided conceptually into thirty-two component parts. This meditation is more a matter of concentration, although it can be very useful in developing the mark of *dukkha*, or unsatisfactoriness. In the traditional Theravada ordination, monks and nuns are introduced to an exercise including five of the thirty-two: hair of the head, hair of the body, nails, teeth and skin. The objective of the meditation is to overcome attachment to the body, and the method is to build a mental picture of each part, to try to see it with the focus of concentrated attention.

If it works (and not everyone can develop the necessary concentration), each part is seen in the mind's eye exactly as it is in reality. The meditation can be utterly fascinating, for the thirty-two parts are merely the start. Once properly developed, it is possible to see all interior organs in whatever detail is desired. It can be like looking through a microscope. The understanding of the body gained through this kind of meditation has often been ahead of the medical science of the day and, in modern times, can be successfully checked against current scientific knowledge. For instance, if you examine with the trained eye of attention eyelashes magnified in great detail, you will discover 'worms called "eye-lickers"' (to quote the books) which live at the base of the eyelash. These 'worms' are well-known to medicine, but are today usually seen through a microscope.

With the eye of meditative attention properly developed, some believe you could do away with artificial aids for medical research. They envisage a science of medicine free from biopsies, free from cutting and slicing. However, few have the capacity to develop the meditation to the necessary depth even if they were interested in its possible medical application. The microscope is a far more accessible and reliable tool, easier to use and faster to learn, than intense concentration that needs protracted development in ideal surroundings.

Another way of setting up mindfulness is through the *asubha* meditations, the meditations on the foul. In the Buddha's day, as in India today, it was not difficult to see corpses in various stages of decomposition. The nine traditional stages range from freshly dead, to bones with some flesh still attached, to bones decayed to powder. A monk would seek out a charnel ground, find a suitable corpse and sit gazing at it until he acquired a clear and stable mental image. He could then leave the cemetery and meditate on the image of the corpse in his own quarters or in the forest, free from disturbance.

To meditate in this way is to reflect on death and decay, thereby to realise that one's own body will also die and be discarded. The exercise is not a morbid preoccupation with death, as some believe. It is an attempt to develop understanding that allows transcendence of physical concerns. The meditator will learn that the body and all physical things are transient and a basis for extreme anguish if there is attachment to them.

Where my teacher trained, in Thailand, a young woman who cooked for the monastery drowned in the river that enclosed the grounds. She had been dearly liked for her sunny disposition and selfless service and many were upset by her death. The abbot, the Venerable Chao Khun Bhavanakosol, had her body placed on a trestle and instructed every meditator in the monastery to file past. They were to try to get a clear mental image of the body, then to go away and meditate on death, the better to come to understand the futility of grasping after material things. It is an uncompromising approach that can work exceedingly well – if the mind is trained in the right way first.

There are various modes of mindfulness that the meditator needs to develop. He has to develop it first 'internally' (being aware of his own body in the various exercises), then 'externally' (being aware of others' bodies), then internally and externally (not at the same time, of course, but serially). Then he needs to develop mindfulness of things as they arise in the body, of things as they pass away in the body, and of things both arising and passing away.

The main point of these different modes of mindfulness is to come directly to understand transience, thereby to undermine craving. It is only possible to crave for – to want strongly – an item or state that is believed to be lasting. If all things are **known** to be as ephemeral as soap bubbles, craving has nowhere to stand. The practice of mindfulness brings transience squarely before the eye of attention, eventually leading to the insight that will eliminate craving entirely. When craving is destroyed in this way, suffering and anguish do not and cannot arise; the goal of freedom from distress is attained.

☆ ☆ ☆

When setting up mindfulness, many meditators lose their motivation when they do not at first succeed in being mindful all day long. You could call them 'those who set out but do not return'. Generally the problem lies not in the motivation but in the manner of practice. Once they apply themselves repeatedly to activities that last no more than five or ten minutes each, their success rate changes markedly. This detailed and systematic approach seems to work for nearly everyone.

The first step is to be mindful internally – in other words, of one's own body and its activities. For this to work, one need not worry about other people, or the externals, but concentrate on becoming mindful and aware of one's own body and its movements. As with any endeavour, success comes with repeated volitions.

We make particular use of something we call 'asynchronous volition'. This is a volition that has a result seconds, minutes or hours later. An analogy would be post-hypnotic suggestion, although in our case we give the order in full consciousness and know exactly why we experience the result.

Asynchronous volition is an unwieldy term for something with which most of us are quite familiar. For instance, many people customarily put in a volition at night to wake at a precise time in the morning. It works every time; they do not expect it to fail. They suddenly regain consciousness and – on checking the clock – find it is exactly the time they had preset. Needing no external alarm clock, they recognise that the mind (or the body) has its own internal one. Their night-time volition takes effect several hours later and is completely reliable.

Setting up mindfulness is based entirely upon the use of asynchronous volition. You say, 'I will be mindful of this activity for the next several minutes,' and then forget all about the volition as such. You forget all about the will to be mindful; you just do it. You pay attention, and the preceding volition carries you through a particular sequence of activities. This avoids the sometimes tortured beginners' attempts to be mindful-of-themselves-being-mindful – which results only in intense self-consciousness and discomfort.

The ideal circumstances to set up mindfulness are found on a residential meditation course. At night before you fall asleep, you say, 'I will get up at five o'clock. I will awake bright, alert and happy.' At the time you make the volition, you may not entirely believe it, but it works. You wake at five. In response to your volition you are alert, reasonably happy and keen to get started.

On a meditation retreat – and at other times, too, if you can remember – the objective is to be aware right through the day from the first moment of waking until you fall asleep at night. It is a tall order but if you break the activities of the day into small segments, it becomes really quite a manageable proposition.

With this approach, your first 'activity' might be from the moment of waking until you get to the bedroom door on your way down to the bathroom. You are aware of moving in bed, turning over, putting your feet out of bed, feet touching the floor. There is pressure, a change of posture to standing, and all the efforts involved. An arm stretches out to get a bathrobe; there are all the movements and sensations involved in putting it on and another change of posture to walking. There are sensations arising in the feet as you walk across the room, and finally there is stretching out to grasp the doorknob preparatory to opening the door.

At that point you stop. You pause, and you retrospect. You look back over that sequence of activities and ask, 'How did I do? Was I mindful right the way through? Were there any gaps?' If there were, you identify them and put in the (asynchronous) volition to do better next time. Do not worry about it. If you have missed – and until you have perfected the practice you can expect to, you just say, 'Right, I'll improve that next time.'

Then you take the next sequence of activities – perhaps down a flight of stairs to a bathroom door. You set out again, and you go as mindfully as you possibly can right the way down the stairs to the door. As your hand grasps the doorknob, you stop. You ask, 'How well did I do? Did I lose it anywhere? If so, what did the mind rush off on to? Do I know? OK, I'll do better next time.' Then you set up the next sequence of activities, and so you go on, right through the day, detailing segments of time no longer than five minutes or ten at the most.

There are a great number of five- and ten-minute slices in a day. A great number of volitions go in to be mindful. A great number of retrospections are done, to assess how well you are getting on. You have checks and balances at all times. It is extraordinarily effective. The reviewing registers the activities you have been engaged in, and if you are doing it even halfway right, success is assured. With that much repetition, you cannot really fail.

I would say, however, that periods of retreat are necessary for those not under full-time training. As most of you have discovered, the first retreat is something of an eye-opener. You realise there is much more to meditation than you had previously thought. A retreat enforces freedom from external distractions and gives you a daily discipline that is hard, if not impossible, to come by any other way. The freedom from distraction and the discipline provide the perfect setting for the development of mindfulness and clear comprehension. As long as you constantly remember to apply yourself to the setting up of mindfulness, progress is assured.

So how can you tell if it is working? With mindfulness practised in this way, you **know** if it is working. You do not have to have anybody to tell you; you know for yourself. Personal knowledge is gained from constantly repeated retrospection and comparison. This leads to great skill in means. You know if you are being more, or less, mindful; you know what the problem areas are. And by constantly renewing the resolve to be mindful, you improve. You cannot help but improve. This works even if you start out doing it wrongly – as many, if not most, people do.

I recall one meditator who was trying this approach with great intensity. His effort was wrong effort; it was accompanied by extreme craving for results. Applying himself very vigorously, his meditation became exceedingly painful, so painful that I could not help feeling sorry for him. He was doing so much retrospection, however, that he saw **for himself** where the problem originated. His mindfulness improved just to the point where he could see where he was going wrong. He re-applied himself, correctly this time and, much to his surprise, it worked. The pains disappeared and the practice began to flow easily. He was able more easily to discern the details of physical activity and a sense of ease and rightness developed.

☆ ☆ ☆

What is the perfection of mindfulness of body? What can it give you? What are its limitations?

Mindfulness of body is perfected when you can observe the arising and passing away of any aspect of body internally and externally. This brings an acceptance of the real nature of the transient body, to the point that craving associated with the body no longer arises.

As an aside, it is important to understand that it is impossible to be aware of all aspects of the body simultaneously. It is impossible to be aware of more than one thing at a time. Even if this is not known from experience, logic shows the impossibility of being aware of everything. There are five physical senses, so through any one we can be aware only of one-fifth of what is going on, physically, around us. That means that 80 percent of potential experience we can never, ever come to know. From the remaining 20 percent, through one sense-base, we then select a fraction of what is available. I wonder just what proportion of potential experience is actually available to us at any time? It is certainly not very much. The most you can experience is only what you can be aware of at any instant. At any instant you can be aware of just one thing: one sensation, one thought, one feeling, one sight, one sound.

With weak mindfulness of body you might be aware of the sensation of 'pressure in a foot'. With strong mindfulness it becomes apparent that 'pressure' is one thing and 'foot' is another. The sensation of pressure is experienced through the sense of touch, which has no visual component. A 'foot' is a visual concept apprehended by eye. They are two different things, experienced separately. While aware of one, it is not possible to be aware of the other. There is only a very limited set of things that you can be aware of at any one time.

This scarcity of objects in the moment means that you can relax. You do not have to strain every fibre of your being, trying to catch every little thing that is going on. You can relax and just pay attention to whatever small slice of experience is occurring at the moment. That takes much of the frustration out of setting up mindfulness.

Mindfulness of body cannot, of itself, lead one to enlightenment; more is needed, namely mindfulness of the other three foundations. So we have: mindfulness of feeling, states of mind and mental objects. Again, we apply the same reasoning to those as we did to body. First internally, then externally, then internally and externally. Then we look at things arising, then at things falling (or passing away), then at things arising and passing away. We have time tonight only to look briefly at these three.

Mindfulness of feeling. There are only three feelings. Many protest immediately when they first hear that, but all feelings are pleasant, unpleasant or neither-pleasant-nor-unpleasant (neutral). Pleasant, unpleasant and neutral feelings are the only kind we deal with through the setting up of mindfulness and **every** feeling in human experience is one of these.

To develop mindfulness of mental states is to set up awareness of the general tone of the mind. It includes the recognition that the mind is happy, sad, scattered, concentrated, lustful, hateful, contracted or tranquil. Most people have some broad idea of whether they are fed up or not. Mindfulness of mental states is the same awareness developed to a higher pitch, so you can distinguish clearly the general tone of the mind according to a set system of classification.

Mindfulness of mental objects is more complicated. It is not, as some believe, mindfulness of the content of thinking. It has nothing to do with the content of thinking, whether rational or imaginary. Mindfulness of mental objects is the clear recognition of patterns of mental behaviour and aspects of experience.

It includes awareness of the presence or absence of each of the five hindrances, of which all meditators have experience even if unable to name them precisely. The five are sensual desire, ill-will, sloth and torpor, flurry and worry (agitation) and doubt. These are obstructive activities that we perform while 'meditating'. Using these, we in effect try to escape from the task of meditation by involving ourselves in a contrary activity. We desire some sensory experience, or develop resentment towards something that happened in the past or might happen in the future; or, failing all else, we fall asleep.

The five *khandha*, or groups of grasping, form another set of mental objects. The five are an exhaustive analysis of everything a human being can experience. They include materiality and four groups of mental experience: feelings, perceptions, volitional activities and consciousness. Each of these groups is mentally grasped at and clung to, hence the translation of the term *khandha* as groups of grasping.

One can divide human experience more finely still, into twelve bases. There is a material base for each sense and a corresponding object: eye and visible object, ear and audible object ... mind and mental object. Practising mindfulness in this way is to be aware of these senses and objects as they arise and pass away. A separate aspect adds the awareness of whatever fetters might arise on each of these bases.

It all sounds very dry when presented in brief like this, but once you get properly started on the meditation, it becomes absolutely fascinating. What kind of fetter might arise on eye-object, for example? We are very attuned to sight. There are any number of visible objects from which to choose. You have only to walk down a street and look in shop windows to have the fetter of craving arise: for that latest gadget, or that latest suit, that beautiful dress, or a CD player you just cannot do without. The fetter arises on eye-object, on the thing seen.

A fetter can arise on the eye rather than the eye-object. For example, eyes may start to deteriorate as you get older. If your arms are not long enough to allow you to read the newspaper and you realise you need glasses, you may find that resentment arises. You resent the fact that your eyes are not as good as they used to be. The fetter of ill-will (resentment) has arisen based on the eye itself.

Another group of mental objects is the seven factors of enlightenment that we have already covered. Developing mindfulness of these is to know whether any of these is present or absent from the mind. Yet another group is the four noble truths. It is possible for these truths to spring to life within one's own being, within one's own meditation. One can experience them to the full. Mindfulness of mental objects includes experiencing the truth of these four: that there is suffering, there is a cause of suffering (namely craving), that suffering can cease altogether and that there is a way leading to that cessation.

☆ ☆ ☆

If you systematically practise the setting up of mindfulness on every task, you will find that your mindfulness increases rapidly. As you are cross-checking yourself every step of the way, you have an actual, objective measure of how well you are doing. You do not need someone else to tell you that you are more mindful than you were. You know it. And you know exactly why.

Being systematic and persistent in developing mindfulness, you become very much more clearly aware of the fact that the mind is given to wool-gathering, say. Moreover, you get to the point where you see that any problem is due solely to lack of correct attentiveness. Not only that, but you begin to realise that the situation is far from hopeless. There is something you can do about it. You know from experience that the practice works because mindfulness is gradually improving as the days and weeks go by. As mindfulness grows, your application to the meditation becomes ever more skilful and effective.

It might take several months – but what are several months after twenty or fifty years or more? It is no time at all, to turn yourself from a wool-gatherer into a supremely mindful being. And you can. Just about anyone can. For apart from a very small number of exceptional cases, success is dependent solely on how much of the right sort of work you care to put in.

Many of you will find that you spend endless ages worrying about how well you are doing. Worry about progress is completely unproductive of anything except suffering; it needs to be restrained. If instead of worrying you had been practising mindfulness, you would be out of the wood, or at least well on the way. The only problem is in becoming sufficiently aware of the worry in the first place to be able to restrain it.

I cannot emphasise enough that this is a method that cannot fail if applied systematically. There is no room in it for prolonged self-pity and other self-indulgences such as depression. Obviously those things occur, as they do for anybody. Everyone is subject to fits of despair and dejection, momentarily and temporarily, until they have solved the problems connected with right application to the meditative path.

As mindfulness grows stronger, the duration of such inefficient states becomes shorter and there develops the capacity to say, 'Oh, that is self-pity. That is despair. That is worry,' in a completely mindful and meditative fashion. Such objectivity negates self-indulgence and allows clear observation of the negative aspects of mind. When this occurs, the arising of an inefficient state loses much of its danger, for it is clearly seen and refused permission to develop into anything harmful. It becomes simply more food for the meditative process.

One begins to see how different states arise and how transient they are. One begins to step aside from one's own involvement in thoughts like, 'Am I making progress?', 'I am a terrible person!' or even, 'I'm the greatest!', and all the other concerns that plague most people from time to time.

If mindfulness is present there is far less chance of being seduced by old patterns of mental or physical behaviour. Life becomes a joy instead of a trial.

☆ ☆ ☆

Setting up mindfulness is central to the entire Buddhist Teaching. You cannot do anything without it. It repays study even at the intellectual level. If you practise it, develop it, it comes to fruition in total freedom from suffering. Knowing all there is to know about the arising and passing away of mind and body, a meditator knows what is possible and what is impossible. Knowing that all compounded things are transient, he cannot regard any such thing as a support for happiness and freedom from suffering. He can no longer be fooled by tales of pots of gold at the end of rainbows. He therefore does not – cannot – crave for any compounded thing. His mind leaps for the unconditioned and he knows, then, the goal of the path. With that the job is done, and he or she is off the wheel of *samsāra*.

8

SPIRITUAL EVOLUTION

I would like to talk tonight about something that every meditator is attempting. The Pali word for the action I have in mind is *bhavanā*. This is often translated as 'mental culture', a term with little if any meaning for most Western people. Trying to reflect the true meaning of mental culture, I have called my talk 'Spiritual Evolution', for that is the objective of the meditative path.

The effort to evolve in a 'spiritual' direction – a direction away from gross attachments to the sensory world – is always founded upon some kind of meditation. People make of meditation a very mysterious and wonderful thing. It is mysterious, I suppose, if you look at it in one way, but in essence meditation is a very simple occupation. It is the attempt to overcome attachment, lust, fear, depression, anxiety, worry and the sense of futility to which many people are prone. It is the attempt to overcome lack of confidence, to overcome things like grief and sorrow, and all the other ills with which man is so familiar. That is what *bhavanā*, mental culture or meditation, is all about.

All would probably agree that these states are unwanted and unwelcome visitors to the mind. You can see by looking around you, and by reflecting on your own experiences, that there are many different ways in which people try to deal with these mental cancers. Curiously enough, even though these mental activities are so common, very few people know much about them. They are certainly not aware that harmful aspects of mind are all based on craving, hatred and ignorance. Most people cannot define clearly what is worry, what is anxiety, what is fear, what is depression. This being so, any attempted remedy is likely to be ineffectual, for neither the complaint nor the remedy is properly understood.

Things like worry, depression and anxiety are not passive states of mind that somehow invade you from outside. They are not things that somehow float around in the environment and that you then 'catch'; they are not things that just happen to you. These states of mind are on the contrary active volitional behaviour patterns. They do not just happen – you 'do' them, you create them. You have to exert energy to create and maintain states of mind such as anxiety and depression. Put simply, people suffer because they choose to. They choose to perform those mental actions. That might be a little hard to take. How could anyone be so foolish as to actively engage in activities that are harmful, deleterious?

A little while ago, I watched a programme on the television that was most instructive in this regard. It was about suicide and paid particular attention to the parents of men and women who had destroyed themselves. The parents were of course grief-stricken, but it went much further than that. Those interviewed were without exception very badly disturbed by their offsprings' suicide – in one case still very much so after nine years; they had nursed the grief, the mental disturbance, the problem, for all that time. It is said that time heals and of course so it does, but it did not seem to make much impact in this particular case.

Why should parents of a child who commits suicide find it so difficult to come to terms with it? One mother, after some months of disturbance and grief, was persuaded by a friend to go horse-riding. She spent an afternoon riding, returning at dusk, and suddenly realised that for the whole afternoon she had forgotten to be disturbed, she had forgotten to grieve. And you know what? She felt guilty – guilty because she had not been suffering. This bereaved mother had forgotten to 'do' grief that afternoon. She had been happy and thought, in retrospect, that it was wrong, that happiness was a bad thing, given her circumstances. Why? It is fairly clear once you track it down.

This society teaches us that we should grieve for the loss of loved ones and dear ones. Fair enough. But it goes further. We are taught at school, and by our very society's conditioning, that there is only one lifetime. We are born, we live and we die and that is the end of it. It does not matter what the Church says: the overriding view and opinion is that there is only one life and at death there is oblivion.

If you take that view and follow it through, it means that any newborn child is a product **entirely** of its parents, both physically and mentally, for it cannot come from anywhere else. There being no life after death there can of course be no life before death, either. That being so, the parents have totally to create that new individual, body and mind. Thus when a child 'goes wrong', as it were, particularly with something so serious as suicide, who is at fault? If you accept the one-life view it is clearly the case that the parents are to blame. It cannot be anybody else's fault. They have created in its entirety a child that has chosen suicide and destroyed itself. It appears that their creation was faulty. No wonder they are upset. One of the most common refrains throughout the television programme was, 'Where did we go wrong?' Not, 'Where did the child go wrong?' but 'Where did we, as parents, go wrong?'

If a child dies of an illness like cancer, then there is no problem. There is no parental guilt attached, because the illness is seen as something coming from outside. It is awarded the same status as a car accident or a murder. An external attack, while regrettable, is quite independent of parental creativity, so it is not a problem. Some argue for the effect of environmental factors on the decision to take one's own life, but that seems to cut little ice with most parents unfortunate enough to have a child who commits suicide. They see that the environmental factors have nothing to work on but the child they produced in its entirety, body and mind. If the child could not withstand the environmental pressures that most of us survive, it has to be their fault for producing a defective individual.

If you contrast attitudes arising from a belief in just one life with those arising from a belief in many lifetimes, with a belief in rebirth or reincarnation, then you find a very different picture. In this case, any child coming into a family is not created in its entirety by the parents – it is a functioning, mature individual in its own right. The child is mature in the sense of having had lifetimes of previous experience. While it unavoidably has to be trained and conditioned to its new environment, it nevertheless brings a great deal of experience and personality with it.

If such a being should later commit suicide, the parents **cannot** believe that it is all their fault because they understand, or at least believe, that their child determines its own way in the world, that it is responsible for its own actions. How can they be as upset? Obviously they would grieve as would any parents, but not to the same excessive degree as those believing the child to be entirely their own creation.

If you choose to believe in the wrong things, then you are going to suffer, you cannot help it: suffering follows inexorably from wrong belief, wrong view. On the other hand, belief in right things, things that are true to fact, ensures that your life is easier and more in tune with reality. Adopting a belief in rebirth, for instance, immediately lessens some of the suffering otherwise associated with suicide.

☆ ☆ ☆

Based on ignorance, based on wrong beliefs, based on wrong views, people perform actions they believe will solve their immediate problems. Even criminal action is based in the same idea. For example, theft is often seen as a way of solving the problem of relative poverty: I do not have something so I go and steal it from somebody who has. It is a very simple outlook for it apparently evens the material balance in the world and would seem – at first glance – to enrich the thief.

The trouble with wrong view is that the correct connections between the action and its final resultant are not seen. The final resultant is most definitely not the acquisition of goods or money. Criminal action might result in the perpetrator being imprisoned, but even this is not the end of the matter. The final result of theft might be to feel guilty during one's lifetime with the additional disadvantage that, on dying, one is likely to be reborn in circumstances considerably worse than those one enjoys now.

If the correct connections between action and resultant are not made, then worsening personal circumstances are inevitable. The wrong kind of action merely aggravates a problem; it leads to greater and greater difficulties. This is true not only for criminal activity but for other kinds of inefficient action as well.

In the Second World War there was a huge quantity of explosives dropped on cities. One bomber pilot said that he believed, with many others, that he was doing the very best thing to solve the immediate problem with which the world was faced. Why was it then that for forty years afterwards he would wake screaming from nightmares about what he had done? There was a conflict between what he believed and what was in fact the action best suited to peace and harmony – at least at the personal level.

Ignorance of the law is no excuse. Although this is normally applied to the legal system, it applies as well to the law of Dhamma, or, more specifically, the law of *kamma*, the law of ethical action and result. Whether you are aware of that law or not, it still operates: how could it be otherwise?

We need to learn of this law for our own and others' welfare. Some of us are alerted to its existence through our own experience; others are introduced to the law of *kamma* through reading about it, or they hear about it when attending meditation classes or lectures such as this. Whatever the source of our information, we have to see for ourselves the operation of the law of ethical action. We need to observe what we do and correlate it with the results we experience. Watched carefully, it becomes clear that selfish actions produce painful consequences while unselfish actions lead to increasing happiness.

If I understand it correctly, one strand of current criminological thinking is that the criminal, if he lands up in prison often enough, will at last decide to go straight. He is supposed to learn through experience that breaking the law results in painful circumstances. The theory is that he will eventually make the connection between his actions and their resultants. Many believe, however, that incarceration must be accompanied by education: there has to be a system of training individuals in what we could call right livelihood.

Seeing the connections between what you do and what you get back afterwards is the essence of the educational system and training that is the eightfold path, the middle way of Buddhism. It is in one sense the whole path, for to see those connections you have to bring in many other things.

The eightfold path is undertaken in essence to seek our own welfare, to get better resultants, not worse. Paradoxically, we find it is only possible to seek our own welfare by increasing and enhancing our concern for other people. We have to think more of others or, at the very least, far less of ourselves. Doing so, it is possible to control and eventually reduce all of the harmful outflows of energy called cankers, corruptions or outflows (*āsava*). We pour energy into mental and physical activities that are harmful to us. If we can stop this, things immediately improve and can go on to improve dramatically. In short, and more simply, if we restrain the so-called normal selfish urges, we become happier as a result.

Followed with dedication the eightfold path ensures a happier life both now and in the future. Such action is a guarantee of a better rebirth. Right across the East the eightfold path is often called the Way to Heaven. The Way to Heaven is a marvellous way; wherever it is found there are also found harmony, love and laughter, prosperity and health – usually in greater degree than where the eightfold path is not followed. The Way to Heaven is worthy of the deepest respect; it is most worthy of being followed. That is why it is called a noble way.

☆ ☆ ☆

If you examine closely the kind of behaviour necessary to follow the eightfold path, you will notice a curious thing. Even this kind of behaviour – being considerate of others and very far from self-seeking – has a selfish component to it. It is still behaviour that is undertaken to solve a problem. People act for the good to make themselves feel better; they do it because they would feel uncomfortable if they did not.

Some help people in difficult situations in order to avoid feeling worthless. I know several people who have worked in a hospice. When asked, they freely admit that if they did not do such work they would feel useless. They help others in order to acquire a feeling of satisfaction; it makes them feel better. Even with good action, the right kind of action, an individual is still trying to solve his immediate problems. In this he is just like the criminal – though it has to be said that the action harms no one at all, unlike actions based in greed and hatred.

If actions are done to right a wrong or to gain a particular benefit, there is always a subtle attachment to the results. Always. Where there is attachment to results there is a problem. If you are unsuccessful you will feel frustrated; if you succeed, you will be disappointed because your very success is never enough. No matter how successful, you find that nothing is perfect, nothing lasts forever.

Consider. You have been working hard for your family or for your partner, either as the breadwinner or houseperson or maybe both. You expect without actually saying so a certain amount of appreciation and consideration. It is only natural; everybody does. Do you get it? Well yes, you do. But is it enough? If you are really honest, never. It is never enough. You want to be appreciated more than you are, to have more consideration than you get. Why?

No matter whether your actions are conventionally good or conventionally bad, you still suffer. If you perform bad actions, you suffer as a bad person suffers. If you perform good actions, you suffer as a good person suffers. Making these connections, making the connections between actions and resultants, is a really crucial step in coming to understand just how we can eliminate things like depression, anxiety, worry, sorrow, fear and the like – that whole ragbag of ills that plagues everyone at some time or another.

Seeing these connections also makes sense of the task of meditation itself. Meditation is undertaken to eliminate suffering of all kinds, completely. Meditation is done to remove totally fear, anxiety, a sense of futility, despair and depression.

☆ ☆ ☆

As every meditator quickly learns, meditation is bedevilled by hindrances. That comes as no surprise at all to you, I know, but have you really tried to define the word? It is easy to use the term hindrances and yet to lose the sense, particularly in English. English is such an object-orientated language that a hindrance sounds like some kind of concrete thing. It is not.

Hindrances are **activities** undertaken by the meditator to solve his immediate problem. Hindrances are not static objects that drop out of the sky, invade you and then go away again as the breeze blows. They are actions that you decide to employ to solve a problem. They are activities designed and undertaken to avoid or remove things like pain, worry, frustration, boredom, anxiety and depression. All hindrances are activities intended to remove states the individual considers negative; instead, they generate further unwanted conditions.

Hindrances cannot have the desired result based as they are in ignorance and blindness. Until the meditator sees the connections between actions and their results, he will not change. He will carry on, figuratively beating his head against a wall. Even the sight of blood does not seem to put many people off. They still religiously continue to beat their heads against an impenetrable wall of hindrances and they suffer as meditators suffer.

I want to look at these hindering activities more closely. They form a large part of any meditator's experience, especially in the early days and quite often for a long time after that. It seems you could probably number a hundred or more kinds, but on examination they can all be divided into five major groups. The five are sensual desire, ill-will, sloth and torpor, flurry and worry and sceptical doubt.

Why would anyone attempting to meditate choose to practise sensual desire instead? Quite simply, they find the meditation **boring**. Not liking the boredom they seek some kind of pleasurable stimulation: they listen to the birds singing or to the traffic going up and down the road, or play with a feeling in the back of the head. They create some kind of diversionary object or activity to focus upon; something that seems to offer more in the way of pleasure and satisfaction – at least in the short term – than does the meditation.

Sensual desire directs the attention through one of the five physical senses or often through the mind itself, building pictures, imagining wonderful things, creating entire wish-fulfilment fantasies; anything rather than the boredom of meditation. While sensual desire may appear to succeed in eliminating distress at the time, it actually aggravates the problem: sensual desire gets stronger and stronger, making the meditation seem more and more boring and unsatisfying. This happens not only in meditation but also in daily life: indulge sensual desire excessively and life itself takes on an air of futility and dissatisfaction.

The connection between sensual desire and its painful results has to be seen and understood before the meditator will endeavour to restrain his continual attempts to escape from dissatisfaction through sensory activity. Either that, or he has to have strong faith or confidence in his teacher's instruction.

What about ill-will, the second of the hindrances? Ill-will is cultivated in response to pain or unsatisfactory conditions. The distress may originate in working life – you remember someone who put you down or upset you in some way – or it may arise in the meditation itself. There are so many potential sources of discomfort: there is pain in the back; you may believe there is too much noise; the room is too hot or too cold; you are too hungry, too full, too tired, too tense, too uncomfortable – the list is endless.

Ill-will is essentially the resentment or anger that arises in response to the painful circumstances. It is a chosen activity of mind that, in common with all the hindrances, can be restrained when its true face is seen. Practising ill-will, the mind is caught up with criticism and resentment of the physical or mental circumstances that you believe upset your equilibrium. Dwelling on all the negative aspects of personal experience predisposes you to see them even more readily and in areas previously free from problems. Practising ill-will, you get more and more bitter and life becomes a weary burden.

Sloth and torpor form the third of the meditative hindrances. What apparent benefit do you think there might be from practising sloth and torpor? I think the name of the hindrance gives it away. People who practise sloth and torpor are in one way or another lazy. They think meditation is a bit too much like hard work and choose instead to rest, to take it easy, to refuse to apply themselves to the setting up of the right conditions for systematic awareness. They seek to meditate without making the attempt to change their habitual behaviour.

This works in two ways. The obvious one is where the meditator is simply lazy and does not want to work hard at anything. The less obvious is where a meditator has established over-effort and over-achieving as habitual patterns of behaviour in all areas of his life. Here the laziness lies in the refusal to restrain the offending habit, and in the mindless continuation of actions sometimes known to be deleterious to the practice.

In both cases there is no effective meditation done. Where under-effort is the problem, the meditator may have a pleasant sleep and wake feeling very refreshed, but no wiser. With over-effort, the meditation is a battleground of tension and pain. At the end of an endless hour, such a meditator will feel wrung out, exhausted and battered, not to mention dazed. It may take him half an hour or so to recover his normal level of intelligence.

The fourth hindrance to the meditation is anxiety or flurry and worry. Why do you perform the action of flurry and worry? Worry, anxiety or planning are always undertaken in an attempt to avoid failure of some kind. You do not want to be found out – and so suffer damage to your reputation. You wish to give a good (and possibly false) impression at some important event in the future. You fear a loss of some kind and worry about how you may avert it. The meditation itself can be a source of worry. You may think you are not getting on fast enough. You think someone might blame you for not working hard enough, for not getting on well enough. Maybe you feel uncomfortable with yourself because you are not succeeding as you think you should. In every case there is fertile ground in which the seeds of anxiety root and grow strong.

There is an endless field for worry if you really want to get down to it. Many people do. They spend ages, hours, even weeks, racked with anxiety, believing that the worry is a constructive attempt to overcome the problems – often completely imaginary – that they face. They have not yet made the right connections between what they do and how they feel. They feel so terrible as a direct result of choosing to expend their energy in this form of mental misbehaviour. They can stop the worry at will, by restraint, but only when they have made the connections – and that takes training in systematic awareness.

There is a fifth hindrance: sceptical doubt. Sceptical doubt is practised when someone finds that the Buddha's Teaching is at variance with the views he holds or the hopes he has. He feels insecure, naturally enough, for one does when one's views are challenged. Feeling unsure, he wants reassurance, he wants – better yet – **proof** that the course he has embarked upon, meditation and the Buddhist way, will solve his problems. He has not yet found that proof so he tries to get it. He starts to analyse, to pull apart, to contrast the Buddhist Teaching with what he believes he already knows. Practical experience is usually a minimal element in this activity, for his existing knowledge comprises a mixture of myth, hearsay and intellectual theorising, providing no firm basis for informed enquiry. Pursuing the path of doubt, he gets into a bigger and bigger tangle. The motive in all this mental activity is to overcome suffering and distress. In common with the other four hindrances, the action of doubting is undertaken in an attempt to solve an immediate problem.

For each hindrance there is a particular perceived problem and an action selected especially to deal with it. These actions, unfortunately, have the wrong results. They aggravate the condition, they hinder the meditation. They hinder the meditation because they set the stage for more frustration, more worry, more anxiety, more boredom, more sleep, more doubt, more pain. This of course is diametrically opposed to the main objective of the meditation practice, which is to reduce and finally eliminate suffering.

A hindrance is not an object, a thing. A hindrance is an activity, an unskilful mental action. It is to pour energy into an unskilful channel of mental behaviour. The energy is wasted, for it simply makes things worse. Whatever temporary relief it appears to give, it does not help one jot in the task of coming to the complete eradication of suffering.

All hindrances are volitional. We choose to do them and, with experience and understanding, can stop doing them. We do need to realise that, however well meant, they produce a greater level of dissatisfaction than existed before. To learn this, we have to make the connections between what we do and the results we experience. We choose to act, we choose to hinder the practice. If we are alert enough, however, if mindfulness is strong and if we make the right connections, we can successfully restrain ourselves from pouring energy into those inefficient, unskilful channels

☆ ☆ ☆

One way to make a really good start at diverting your energy away from unskilful channels is to learn to be even-minded about the things you would normally classify as problems. To achieve this is extremely difficult at first. When alerted to a problem you observe but **do nothing about it**, though every fibre of your being cries out to 'fix' it before it is too late. It needs heroic restraint and you have to have faith. You have to say, 'I guess it will turn out all right. I will not interfere.'

Developing faith or confidence in the meditation, we learn to say, 'I will not interfere, I'll just let it be, I will not get upset about it.' As a result, we begin to see clearly that suffering is caused by our actions to overcome things like painful feelings, imagined dangers and imagined losses. It is the **action** that causes the problem, not the painful feeling. It is not the imagined disaster that causes the problem – it is our reaction to that imagined disaster. It is not the painful feeling – it is our action taken to deal with the painful feeling that is the problem. The actions we choose to undertake are of various kinds: worry, depression, anxiety, anger, sensual desire and many more. They are all activities of mind that require effort. No matter how much they may seem to happen 'by themselves', the truth is that we 'do' them; we have to work at them.

If you see the connections between unskilful actions and their painful results then – and then only – can you restrain the actions. At this stage in meditation, when you have made those connections, when you begin to restrain these actions, a beautiful thing happens. A sense of wonder fills the mind and the meditation suddenly becomes spacious, calm and seemingly effortless. You feel as though you do not have to try any more. A sharp clarity develops and a sense of profound peace and of being in the right place. It is a wonderful experience.

A sense of deep peacefulness comes to be not only in the meditation but also in daily life, for the two are inextricably linked. Problems seem less important, and there begins to develop one of the most valuable attributes anyone can ever have: the ability to laugh at oneself. As the meditation unfolds, it becomes impossible not to, when you see how much effort you have poured into activities that are stupid, even crazy. There is, in addition, a great sense of relief when you realise that you do not have to do it any more.

Life lives far more harmoniously if we stop interfering with it. We see that all our attempts to solve problems have really made them worse. What a discovery that is! And what a relief! It means it is not necessary to take things so seriously. It means that we can relax a bit, that we can enjoy life, rather than feeling we have to struggle so much, or that we have to worry all the time.

Of course this does not mark the end of the road. There is much more to do. The hindrances have not been totally overcome, but at least you know where you are going. You have seen how it can be, you know the sort of thing you have to do, or rather the things you have **not** to do. It is a tremendous blessing, a benediction, because at last you know which path to take. You know which actions are likely to be effective and which are not.

Life gets lighter, brighter, more enjoyable, and a sense of peace, harmony and a kind of excitement, a joy in living, begin to make themselves known. Life seems worthwhile for its own sake, not for what 'I' get out of it. Things have changed markedly from the self-centred attitudes that accompanied one's early efforts.

This is what *bhavanā*, mental culture or spiritual evolution, is all about: not adding things to ourselves but getting rid of those actions that have unpleasant results and that we previously chose to do. First we get rid of grossly unskilful actions like murder, theft, adultery, harsh and untruthful speech and intoxication. This allows the possibility of meditation. Through meditation we get rid of unskilful **mental** actions – the hindrances – and discover as a result that life is beautiful. Eventually we remove psychological dependence on anything at all, and reach journey's end, enlightenment, *nibbāna*.

9

THE TOTALITY OF COMPASSION

Once upon a time there lived a young woman whose earnest desire was for a perfect relationship. One summer's day she met a man. They fell in love and began an adventure of love and romance together. She was ecstatically happy; she had found what she was always looking for. In her happiness, she would tell the birds, the flowers, the trees – anyone – about this most perfect relationship that she had found.

As time passed, though, a curious thing began to happen. The man she had met, her prince, became somehow less attractive, he became even ugly; and she began to suspect that he had used unfair means to charm her into his embrace. As this suspicion grew, things got worse between them. They got worse and worse until in the end – with many sighs, with many tears and much sorrow – she felt she had to say goodbye to this erstwhile prince and turn instead to the embrace of solitude.

As fate would have it, it was not long before there was a knock at the door of her flat and there, on the doorstep, was a man who had been told – wrongly – that the flat was now for sale. It was love at first sight. She embarked upon another adventure of love, passion and romance, convinced that this time it was the real thing.

The years passed and the princes came and went. Her disappointment grew and grew. Bemoaning her lot, she began to wonder why it was that she was singled out for this treatment. Could all men be so bad as she was finding them? Sorrowfully, she pondered and grieved. Gradually, her suspicions hardened. Not all men, surely, could be as dastardly as she was painting them. Perhaps she too had a part to play in this. She began to wonder if it might even be all her fault.

Questioning her own behaviour, she embarked upon a process of self-examination and self-enquiry that marked the beginning of a great adventure. She set out on the true adventure into relationship, to discover what it really means.

☆ ☆ ☆

This story in various forms has been constantly repeated since time began. It has been repeated with romance, with jobs, with friends, with families. It has been repeated in a million and one different ways, and illustrates an important truth that I want to talk about tonight.

That truth is this: any withdrawal from reality is balanced by corresponding pain and distress. Any escapism creates its own pain, creates its own problems. There are two different kinds of escapism or withdrawal: creative escapism and destructive escapism. Both have the same outcome. Escapism is refusing to acknowledge reality by constructing for yourself an alternative version you would prefer.

The creative variety of escapism may be always to wish for and fantasise about the perfect relationship. You may construct an ongoing fantasy about seeking a soulmate, wondering if each new person you meet is the one you have been looking for these many lifetimes. You may create a fantasy at a much lower level, based on an urgent need for sexual fulfilment. Your dream is to relate sexually to another in a positive, dynamic and wholly satisfying way, all the time. I ask you: how often does that ever happen, all the time? And yet the fantasy, the escapist dream, is seldom far from the mind. Escapist fantasies are extraordinarily compelling.

You may have a positive creative fantasy, an escapism, in which every move you make is imbued with deep meaning and significance. Every person who crosses your path you are somehow 'fated' to meet; you have deep karmic ties with them and things to 'work out'. Every cat that crosses your path has deep symbolic meaning. Every crow that flies past is an omen of great significance. People live these fantasies, they really do. It is escapism, pure and simple. If you consider every event fateful in this way, then watch out, for you are escaping from reality in what one might call a mythical way. You are making of life a sort of dungeons-and-dragons game, when the truth is far different.

At first sight, the destructive fantasy, destructive escapism, is of quite a different kind. Here you see intrigue, powermongering and backstabbing everywhere. Wherever you look, you see hatred, criticism, evil designs and conspiracy. People are always ready in this kind of escapism to believe that they are being blamed or criticised, to believe that they are the target of other people's actions, to believe that the world is out to get them. Paranoid fantasy at this level is surprisingly common. It is really a form of escapism from the anonymity and loneliness of the everyday. As such it has its roots in the same place as the positive variety of escapist fantasy.

Destructive escapism differs from the creative kind in that here there is no love: there is only vicious self interest masked behind smiles and good manners. I know a man who, if someone is pleasant to him, gets extremely worried. He has taught himself that when someone smiles and is accommodating it means he is preparing to slip in the knife. A kind word or a smile immediately puts him on the defensive. He immediately becomes suspicious, wondering what they want or in what way they are out to get him. A negative escapism.

Whether creative or destructive, escapism is the creation of an imaginary picture that is real only to you. The fantasy is real enough to you but it is real only to you. It is not real to everybody else; it may not be real to anybody else. One thing is certain: it is not a correct picture of things as they are.

Escapism, withdrawal from reality, allows no meditative equanimity at all. Such escapes are always extremely positive or extremely negative; they do not have a midway point. They generate no insight at all. No matter what the omens may say, no matter how many crows fly by, it is still the same old life, the same old reality.

If someone persists in these escapes, what happens? If he persists in withdrawing from reality in this way, what is the result, what is the outcome? With either the creative kind of fantasy or the destructive kind, his suffering, his distress, increases and increases. Creative escapism when indulged constantly results in normal life becoming more and more meaningless and futile. With destructive escapism, life seems more and more bitter and dangerous. Either way suffering increases and increases.

As times passes, suffering grows to the point where enquiry begins. It can take a long time, lifetimes even, but eventually distress grows to the point where you come to believe that there must be more to life than you see at the moment. You begin to ask yourself why things are so unsatisfactory. Eventually, just like the young woman in the story, you come to suspect that it is you who are at fault, not the world. That recognition is the beginning of wisdom, the beginning of compassion.

You may decide that meditation is the supreme method for coming back to reality, for restraining your escapism, for turning away from escapes to which you have become habituated over the years. You may believe that it will painlessly solve all your problems. But awareness of suffering has only just begun with the task of meditation. As those of you who have been meditating for some time know well, the awareness of suffering that arises with continued practice is enhanced, not diminished. There is a very good reason for this. It lies in the way meditation works.

☆ ☆ ☆

Just how does meditation turn you from an escapist into someone who is prepared to face reality directly? How does it do it? You start to meditate, and what are you told to do? To pay attention to things as they are – not just in the seated practice for half an hour a day, but in every conscious moment as far as you are able. You are instructed to be in the present, to be with what is happening. By implication that means coming away from the fantastic, from the escapist world you may have been living in.

You begin to learn, if you do this, that there are many different responses to events. You begin to learn further that those responses are not automatic. Your actions do not just happen – they are under your control, if you are aware of what is going on. It is a huge 'if', but to discover that you are responsible for what you do is a most wonderful thing, for it makes you captain of your own ship. You have power over your life where previously you may have been at the mercy of every omen or whisper.

All relative things are conditioned and some relative phenomena condition others. Any action or any deliberate response is a volitional act. It is something done by yourself, chosen by yourself, willed to happen by yourself. You may as yet be unconscious of it but it is nevertheless a volitional action, as, mark you, is ignore-ance itself. The root cause of all our problems is ignorance (ignore-ance). To ignore something, we have first to be aware of its existence. Recognising something we do not like, we then turn away from it mentally; we ignore it. We are aware of what is going on, but choose to hide it from ourselves.

Any act, any response you make to life, is volitional. You choose it. It having been chosen, you can if you wish stop it, modify it or restrain it. But first you have to become conscious of it. As an aside, the whole reason for rules in the meditative training is to enable you to become conscious of your acts, your responses, your actions, your volitional movements of mind and body.

Let us look at various problems to examine how non-meditators respond and, in contrast, how meditators respond if they are doing their job properly. There are just three ways of dealing with a problem. If you find yourself in difficult circumstances, these are the three things that can happen. You might decide that other people are at fault or lacking in some way. You might decide that you yourself are lacking or at fault in some way. Thirdly, if you are meditating properly, you will simply observe the rise and fall of events, being aware that as one thing arises, so another one falls.

Relationships are always fertile ground for all kinds of upsets. Say you have a difficult partner or a difficult colleague, someone with whom you are closely associated. The relationship between you has grown painful, difficult, awkward and full of friction. What kinds of attitudes, what kinds of responses might there be?

In the first case, you decide that the other person is entirely in the wrong. You know he has to be told, and that it is your responsibility to make him aware of where he is going wrong. You exert yourself heroically in the attempt to straighten him out so harmony can reign again, never doubting that you are in the right. It is like enforcing peace at the point of a gun – it does work, sort of, but it does not really solve any problems.

Alternatively, you decide that if the relationship's going sour, it must be you yourself who is at fault. You examine your own behaviour and your own motives for faults, for errors and omissions. You attempt to adjust your own actions, your very character, to ensure harmony, and may try to force yourself into a wholly unnatural mould. Such constant self-blame is just as damaging as always placing the blame for disharmony on another.

In contrast to both the preceding examples, the meditative response is to recognise that dependent upon certain things other things arise. It is to see the interplay of conditioning, to see the interplay of characteristics, and not get caught up in the passions that so easily arise in close contact with other human beings. It is cool and collected, recognising faults where they exist, but not getting enmeshed in concepts of fairness and justice. Meditation is built upon the calm observation of what is present, which among other things implies a mature acceptance of differences between people.

Attending a residential meditation course can for some provoke a rich variety of problems of the escapist kind. One might think initially that there is not much scope for sensual desire on a retreat – after all, the setting is fairly austere – but it is the very austerity that provokes the problem.

Desire arises for comfort. Desire arises to linger in a hot bath, to have fresh clothing and clean sheets. Desire arises for company, to be able to talk to people, for conversation and sympathy. Craving for more food is not uncommon, though there is in reality plenty. All these things are sensual desire. You might even find a desire for solitude arises because you know that when you are alone you can relax and not worry about how you appear to others. Even here, you are seeking comfort. Sensual desire arises so easily in austere circumstances.

What sort of response might there be to sensual desire on a residential meditation course? There are three, just as before.

Some people break the rules to get what they want. In their view it is simple: you want something, you take immediate steps to get it. You never question why there is a rule forbidding something; all you know is that it stands in the way of what you want. You break the rule to satisfy your desire. It happens all the time. It is seldom recognised that in breaking a rule there is lost an opportunity to learn something about yourself. Having transgressed, such people will usually try to justify their actions. They will explain to themselves and the instructor that they need this or that particular thing to keep themselves on an even keel so they can meditate properly. They have missed the point entirely.

Others shun indulgence like the plague. When sensual desire arises, they try everything in their power to crush it. In contrast with their more indulgent fellows, they become far too ascetic.

One outcome of this leaning is the desire for greater discipline. They want more rules. They want **better** rules. They want a schedule that tells them what they should be doing every second of the day, thinking that only in this way can they avoid the clutches of sensual desire.

The common theme here is the belief that the retreat centre is to blame for the difficulty. The first meditator says quite definitely that the environment is at fault; it is not giving him what he needs, so he goes and gets it anyway. The second says that he is not able to apply himself properly because the rules are not rigorous enough, so the place is at fault. Both usually lose no time in pointing this out and, especially in the case of meditators who want more aggressive austerity, complain that they are being inadequately taught.

The individual who blames only himself when things go awry is in a difficult position. Unable to believe that the environment is at fault, he may conclude that he is unequal to the task. Always ready to assume his own inadequacy, he seldom if ever stops to think that, being human, he cannot be so different from everyone else. With sensitive instruction, this problem is usually overcome fairly easily. If the view of personal inadequacy is deeply entrenched, however, it is a different matter.

The self-blamer is not to be confused with one who always has what he or she believes to be a perfectly valid reason for a problem claimed to be intractable. This kind of meditator usually maintains adamantly that his or her circumstances are special, and that the meditation teacher is not making sufficient allowance for the unique nature of his or her peculiar experience. As such, they fall into the first group – those who believe the environment is at fault.

Only the third person, the true meditator, has the right grasp of the matter. The true meditator recognises that sensual desire arises because he or she is ignoring an aspect of immediate reality. This shows most commonly as boredom with the meditation, what the books call 'boredom with the profitable'. There may be a refusal to acknowledge that things are transient, resulting in a perception of meditation as stultifying. Sensual desire may arise on a feeling of hunger or a twinge of pain in the legs. It may arise based on a refusal to accept a particular facet – say craving – of his or her own nature, or on the feeling of warmth caused by sitting in the sun.

A skilled meditator tries very hard to be more mindful and does that most sensible of all things: restrains sensory activity wherever possible. Such a person does not let the mind go out to imagine, to fantasise, to escape into dreams of more food, more comfort, hot baths, romantic interludes or foreign holidays. The true meditator realises that dreams of mountain caves, total austerity or other meditation systems are a snare and likewise to be restrained. He or she keeps the mind pinned down to the moment, to the job in hand, and guards the senses from indulgence in their objects.

Some, instead of being troubled by sensual desire, find that their meditation is a battleground of ill-will. As a gross generalisation, you can say that all meditators desire one of two things: comfort or progress. You either want progress or you want comfort, and you are not too concerned about the opposite pole. If either of these desires is frustrated, ill-will or hatred arises, and there is hostility towards the supposed obstacle. The hostility is directed at the thing that you believe to be blocking the fulfilment of your desire for comfort or progress.

Some hate the place, the conditions, the rules and other people in the environment. Based on this, they fall into wrong action – wrong action of body, wrong action of speech, wrong action of mind. In other words, when frustrated, they perform actions based upon hatred. When this happens, much criticism is heard, much nagging, much talebearing, much backbiting. The situation can escalate into a very unpleasant time for everyone close to the meditator practising hatred in this way.

Others, recognising that the environment is not to blame for their frustration, blame themselves instead. They conclude that they are not working hard enough, they are not keen enough, their mindfulness is not good enough. Judging their efforts as seriously flawed, they hate themselves for it and fall into wrong action of body, of speech and of mind. They castigate themselves for being weak, for inadequate effort, for not being able to progress in the way they know they should.

In contrast, the true meditator knows that ill-will arises on ignore-ance and takes steps to restrain the mind. He or she does not allow indulgence in negative thinking, does not allow resentment to build, but tries to be more mindful in the right way.

The more you try to escape from a problem, the more painful

things get. It is an inevitable progression. Eventually the pain will force you to be mindful of things as they are. Then, things as they are can be summed up in one word: painful.

Through increasing efforts to escape in the wrong ways, we become increasingly aware of the first noble truth: that things are painful, that life is painful, that there is indeed suffering and distress. Our actions and their results force us to take note of the first truth whether we like it or not.

In short, no matter what we do, we find ourselves still on the path. There is really no escape from the path, for the further we stray from paying attention to things as they are, the more we increase our pain and distress to the point where it cannot be ignored any longer. The distress drives us back in on ourselves, back to paying attention to things as they are. With increasing mindfulness, the suffering lessens, and as suffering lessens, Dhamma, the law of life, is seen more clearly. As the law of life is seen more clearly, wisdom grows.

Following this line of enquiry to its limits, you will realise that there can be no eternal hell. The deeper you dig yourself into hell states, the more painful it gets, until a point is reached where you cannot ignore the pain – **and its causes** – any more. You then start attending to things as they are, and with that you turn yourself around and start heading in the direction of freedom.

That being so, no one can ever be an impossible case. I do not care how bad you think you are or may have been. I do not care how terrible the actions you have done. I do not care how dull you think you are. I do not care how weak you think you may be. None of these things is in the last analysis at all relevant. All you have to do is keep on living your life in the way you think best. If you choose the wrong path, suffering will increase. As the pain increases, you will be forced to take note of it and will seek a way to ease your discomfort. Eventually you will find the only secure way to eliminate pain and distress, and that is to eradicate craving by eradicating ignore-ance.

To complete the picture, it has to be said that there is no lasting heaven state either, for the same arguments apply. If you wonder how it is that pleasant, heavenly states could ever be considered painful, we have to broaden our definition. The 'pain' in this case is a question of unsatisfactoriness: the pleasant states do not last and need constant and tiresome work to reinstate and maintain. There is, in short, no rest possible even within the heaven realms. They are not the true freedom that we all seek. True freedom lies quite beyond; beyond all relative phenomena both pleasant and painful, good and evil, light and dark. It is indescribable and yet it is always here and now. We are all seeking nothing less.

No one can ever lose their way permanently, for the very law of life guides us ever towards the way to freedom. You could say that the universe is totally compassionate, which is why I have called my talk 'The Totality of Compassion'.

10

DEVELOPING POWER
OVER THE HINDRANCES

If you look closely at any powerful person, you will find someone who is determined to have things his own way. You will find someone who is determined to ensure, if at all possible, that his environment will conform to his own wishes. Such a person does not want to change himself to fit in with his surroundings; he wants to dominate them. He wants to be in control.

A person is powerful when he can get what he wants most of the time. A person is seen by others to be powerful if he can get what other people want. Power is the ability to acquire the things most people want. They want many possessions, fine clothes, wealth, houses, cars, yachts and playthings. To be rich enough to afford these things is to be powerful. People want to be famous. To be known by many others, to have your name up in lights or constantly in the media is to be powerful.

The ascetic is an individual who desires the power of self-control and is prepared to subject himself to great stresses to bring about his chosen objective. He desires power over his own body, rather than over the external environment.

Those who truly serve their fellows, no matter in what capacity, desire power over the suffering of other people; they wish to alleviate or eliminate the distress in the world. They desire power over the external environment for the welfare of other people and are prepared to sacrifice their personal comforts to acquire it.

There is a common feature in all these various desires, in any desire. No matter who you are, if you want something, you experience that common feature, for it operates for everyone.

Consider your own life. What is most prominent when you seem unable to get the things you want? It is dissatisfaction; it is distress at your inability to control your universe to get what you want. The dissatisfaction may have tinges of resentment or anger. You may get depressed or envious of others. You may experience self-pity. Even so, the most significant aspect of mind is, without a doubt, dissatisfaction. This is the thing that you are attempting to get rid of by seeking power. Of course you seek power to get what you want. Of course you seek power to change your circumstances. But, in truth, you seek power to eradicate dissatisfaction.

Everyone has some definite skills and abilities. Owing to the boundless diversity of past experience, these skills and abilities vary from person to person, but all have been brought into being through desires nurtured over years and over lifetimes.

Someone who has wanted always to win at any cost will have developed qualities and attitudes of mind that enable him to come out on top in almost any competitive encounter. He or she may be very aggressive and self-confident. His ruthlessness may be legend. He may be very devious. His character, his set of behaviour patterns, has been developed to ensure that he gets what he wants – to win – as often as possible. It is not in question whether the qualities are good or bad. It is enough that they work most of the time.

Someone who has sought to be famous will have developed definite 'people skills'. He or she will have nurtured the capacity to relate well to other people simply to become well-known. Such an individual does not necessarily have to be popular; it is enough that he comes before the public eye in an unforgettable manner. He may upset many people while pleasing many others. That is of no concern; he still becomes famous.

Aiming at 'success' in Western terms, an individual will develop the capacity to work with great energy. Taught by his elders that anything can be achieved with enough hard work, he may have been strongly conditioned to over-achievement. For many, this attitude has been reinforced by criticism every time they sought to do something that did not produce a tangible object. These unfortunates would never have been allowed to sit around 'doing nothing', for example, and consequently find that they cannot relax very easily.

These ways of behaving become so familiar to us that, as adults, we seldom notice them. They have become habitual, unconscious. They are the way we are, and are never questioned. We use them all the time but never really know it. They are our skills; the activities that are the easiest to employ just because they are the most familiar and habitually used. Such skills become for each of us the line of least resistance, the 'easy way out' of difficult situations, even though they may appear effortful to others.

We seek power that we may allay dissatisfaction but find that it does not work as well as we would wish. The eradication of suffering is not so easy a matter as simply acquiring the ability to alter one's environment. If that were the case, then the rich would always be happy and the famous could never commit suicide.

Many, through lack of ability or opportunity, have no hope of acquiring power through conventional means. Though clearly aware of dissatisfaction, their choices are limited when trying to alleviate it. Caught perhaps in the poverty trap, embroiled in warfare or trapped in an environment where famine is rife, they can do little to ensure their own physical welfare; they are powerless. Some, conventionally successful and owning property, wealth and social standing, and therefore possessing the power to control to some extent their own lives, come to realise that none of their success is entirely effective in removing dissatisfaction.

The oppressed and downtrodden see no hope of obtaining satisfaction through the 'normal' channels of health, wealth and community; the wealthy wonder where next they can turn, having tried nearly everything that we are taught should produce happiness. In either case, this presents a dilemma, for orthodox methods of seeking happiness have to be abandoned and remaining avenues of exploration in search of that elusive peace of mind may seem outlandish or strange in the modern intellectual climate.

When all else fails, yet still desperate for an answer to life's ills, people try any avenue that might offer some hope of release or a clue to the mystery of our purpose on this earth. Some turn to New Age activities. Some turn to religion. Some turn to the meditative path. Their dissatisfaction drives them always to search for something that may help to reduce the emptiness they sense at the heart of their existence.

Most people, when they first come to meditation, have strange notions about what it will do for them. A few believe that meditation may provide the key to unlimited sensual satisfaction. Others think that they may be able to get totally relaxed, this being what they desire most after the stresses of day-to-day living. Others hope that meditation may confer miraculous abilities. Many desire only a more comfortable existence. A few seek in meditation an end to distress, having tried everything else and found it wanting.

So people come to meditation. They come at almost any age; they come for almost any apparent reason – but they all have two things in common. All find life unsatisfactory; all bring with them skills developed over years and years of living.

If, by the way, you would claim that you do not suffer, that your life is perfectly all right and that there is nothing wrong at all, then I would suggest that you look again. No one takes up a discipline like meditation unless they think that it is going to give them something they do not have at present. They feel something is missing. To that extent, they find life unsatisfactory.

The first steps in meditation, often to the surprise of those grown used to contemporary permissiveness, are all concerned with morality or, more accurately, ethical behaviour. If the meditation is to succeed, then it is necessary that the mind be as calm as is reasonably possible before the attempt. This can only be so if actions making for guilt, fear, shame and anxiety are expunged from one's repertoire of behaviour patterns. Of course it is not quite this simple and instead of talking of eradication at this stage, we are really talking of a more fundamental restraint of behaviour. This demands a definite and determined attentiveness to activity of all kinds, for it is surprising how often non-meditators act unconsciously in ways that are extremely inefficient. The five precepts, which some regard as a little quaint, are a prescription for behaviour that will assure the best conditions for a seeker to find the path to total liberation.

After regulating your external behaviour, the next step in the meditative training is to purify the mind. You attempt to come to a state of watchful attention that is unhindered by such things as prejudice, bias, craving, hatred and dullness. This watchful state, sometimes called bare attention, is also known as access or momentary concentration. The mind in this state is pure and free from hindrances to observation.

If you constantly return your attention to a single object or process, such as the rise and fall of the abdomen, the mind will eventually settle down. It will give up its waywardness. It will give up its constant flightiness and agitation or its dullness and confusion. The attempt is to be made gently and repetitively. The use of force is completely counterproductive and needs to be avoided. There has to be the right kind of effort as opposed to the wrong kind. Only when all is correctly in balance can purity of mind be found. Only then is the mind in a fit state to see what is really going on. There are a few major obstacles to the process, however.

Consider your life until the time when you started meditating. What did you do to ensure that you succeeded in your chosen tasks? What qualities of mind and behaviour did you employ to get the best out of life? How did you deal with the problem of pain and frustration? What happened when things got a little too much?

To become successful, have you been hard-working, honest, trustworthy, loyal, determined, considerate and trusting? Or did you employ other tactics to get what you wanted? Are you someone who used qualities like deception, laziness, pretended illness, selfishness, theft, violence, threats or temper tantrums to achieve your immediate goals? How did you behave before you took up the practice of meditation?

Whatever you used to do before you came to meditation, the chances are that you are doing it still.

Are you the sort of person who finds it easy to see faults? Do you readily criticise weakness, whether in other people or in yourself? If you do, then you have developed a definite skill in perceiving the negative side of life, and this tends to make you dour and pessimistic regarding both yourself and those around you.

Or are you someone who sees only the good things? Do you describe all your acquaintances as 'the best' or 'the most brilliant' at the particular things they do? Do you refuse to see genuine faults, believing somehow that in this way you make the world a better place in which to live? If you do, you have developed a skill in seeing the world 'through rose-coloured spectacles' and your judgment cannot be trusted.

Perhaps you unquestioningly imitate what other people do. Perhaps you follow the herd, having found in the past that it gave you a degree of safety and security. There are definite dangers in doing this, for those whom you follow may not do what is right for you personally. Scientific research done on this urge to follow has yielded some frightening results. Ordinary men and women have been induced to give to a 'patient' (an actor) an electric shock they firmly believed to be fatal. They were prepared to suspend their own judgement and kill another human being just because someone said that it was the right thing to do.

Whatever you used to do before you came to meditation, the chances are that you are doing it still.

The ways in which you deal with your world were developed because, at the time and in the circumstances, they worked. Both positive and negative qualities of mind can be used to get you what you want. The only difference between them is that the negative kinds of behaviour have an outcome that is eventually painful. They carry a built-in danger factor from which there is no escape.

When you come to the practice of meditation, you try your best to follow the instructions given by the meditation teacher. Naturally you do not succeed straight away in purifying the mind; it is not an easy task. There are hindrances to overcome.

What are these hindrances? They are habits, nothing more, nothing less. Hindrances are the ways in which you have conditioned yourself to deal with your universe. They are the very skills, positive and negative, that you have developed during your long years of living.

If you have learned to work hard to get what you want in the world, then you will work hard to get success in meditation. You will exert great force to succeed. Because of this you will fail, for meditation does not respond to the use of excessive force. It needs gentleness. Using force, you become agitated, tense and self-critical. Being agitated and tense, it is not possible for the mind to quieten enough to see what is happening and purity of mind is far, far away.

You might have always preferred to take things easy. You might like always to relax and be comfortable, having found that this approach generally gets you what you want. In meditation, however, it really does not work. Attachment to comfort and sensuality, attachment to ease and relaxation, ensures that you will never achieve success at the task of meditation. The hindrances of sensual desire and sloth and torpor are yours because you have worked to develop them in the past, when seeking an end to distress and dissatisfaction. They may have been very useful then, but when it comes to meditation, they are a great obstacle.

Another common kind of behaviour is planning and worry. There is no doubt that the ability to look forward to what might happen is a valuable skill in the normal, work-a-day world. In meditation, though, it is a major problem, for the speculative mind is never quiet. It is always full of anxieties and agitations. It is unable to come to the calmness and purity needed for clear observation.

Notice that all these ways of using and conserving energy are skills that were developed a long time ago. They were used to cope with life in what was the best way at the time. The skills have been practised to the point where they operate almost automatically. They are unquestionably the easiest to use simply because they are already in existence. They do not have to be created especially for the occasion.

If a meditator is off guard, if he is less than careful about the way he approaches the practice, he will naturally attempt to use his existing skills to get what he wants. He will slip automatically into old habits and attempt to establish purity of mind by overwhelming the recalcitrant mind with effort, or by analysis and planning, or by indulging in comfortable relaxation. Doing this, all manner of discomfort and further hindrances arise, simply because of the inappropriate efforts. The **idea** of bare attention has become more important than the practice of it and the meditator has become blinded by this image. He has fallen back on old ways of doing things. He has fallen asleep, in a sense, and is no longer in charge of his meditation. He is indulging in habitual behaviour.

☆ ☆ ☆

You can see some instructive things on residential courses. You might be surprised at the number of people who simply imitate what someone else does, right or wrong. If someone talks during a period of silence, another imitates and soon there are several people talking and the meditative atmosphere is completely lost.

Perhaps a meditator will break a minor rule, quite knowingly, but on the assumption that, 'Surely it wouldn't matter just this once ...' Someone else sees the infraction and thinks, 'Well! If she can do it, then so can I.' Before you know what is happening there is an epidemic of rule-breaking and the smooth running of the place and the meditation are both temporarily upset.

You can also tell a great deal about someone's habits just by looking at their body language. While sight is not an infallible guide to the way in which a person is coping with what is happening, it can often show clearly what sort of mental state is in existence.

Those who appear physically rigid, with signs of unnatural strain on the face and in the set of the shoulders, are probably accustomed to exerting great effort to get what they want out of life. They have not yet learned that this excessive energy does not bring success in the meditation practice.

A variation on this theme is the rigidly tense individual who also suffers from twitches. The eyes may never be still, even during the meditation, let alone when walking around the garden. The body may jerk spasmodically. This is often a sign of excessive exertion combined with an habitual anxiety or worry pattern. These people find it difficult to stop the thinking and planning thoughts that arise whenever they try to do something new or whenever life gets uncomfortable. As life is uncomfortable most of the time, given their excessive efforts, they are in a bit of a fix.

At the opposite end of the spectrum, someone who is constantly leaning over at a seemingly impossible angle during the seated practice is without question suffering from an attack of sloth.

There are those who fall somewhere between the two extremes but who still have not got it quite right. Some try to help the meditation along by controlling the rate of their breathing, producing some amazing contortions of the abdomen; others seem to find it necessary to move the head rhythmically to accentuate the rise and fall.

These visual impressions can tell one a lot about the habit patterns a particular meditator has to deal with. It is obvious, too, that those who follow the instruction and attempt to keep the body still, without interference, have an easier time of it than those who are not so disciplined.

In every case of misapplied effort, the meditator is trying to achieve power over the mind by using techniques that cannot work. He is treating bare attention as though it were just another worldly goal. Doing this, he cannot avoid falling into his habitual ways of behaving, for there is not enough attentiveness to avoid it. He or she has forgotten, or never really realised, that meditation is not so much doing something but more **refraining from** doing that which is habitual. To meditate is to be mindful and self-possessed at all times. This could be called the secret of meditation, for it is not so easily learned.

☆ ☆ ☆

All hindrances have two faces. On the one hand, they arise automatically as a tendency to action. On the other hand, they are performed, by choice and with intent, as volitional action now.

The tendency arises because of past conditioning. You have reacted to similar frustrations in the past in just this way and this has predisposed you to act in the same manner now. The tendency is not at this point action, however. It is like a doorway that arises in the mind. Over the door is written 'worry', for example, and through that open door you can see the whole field of worry that you could walk into if you chose.

At this time you are very much on this, the safe side, of the doorway. You definitely have the choice as to whether or not you enter the domain of the hindrance. Of course, because you are in the habit of going through that particular door, you may well do so now – but you do not have to. You can say to yourself, 'I don't think I want to play that game today.' You can turn away and continue your meditative journey. If you do go through the door and enter the hindrance's sphere of influence, it is still possible – though **much** more difficult – to turn around and come out again. It is definitely easier not to enter in the first place.

Given enough time and sufficient refusals to go through the various doors, you will find that even the **tendencies** towards those actions begin to get weaker. It does not happen all at once and it does take time – but it definitely does work. It becomes easier and easier to uncover the purity of mind that is always there.

Initially, purity of mind is very tender and in danger of being upset at any time by the hindrances. It is not possible to maintain it for as long as one would wish. It is too near to the obstructions. It is too easily broken up.

To overcome this problem, it at first seems natural to deepen the concentration and thus suppress more firmly those things that agitate the mind even slightly. This is the path of concentration meditation – also known as the way of control. It demands great vigilance of mind. You sit there hawk-eyed, ready for any disturbance that might appear. When it does you immediately eliminate it, not allowing it to grow to any dangerous size. You cut down everything that arises above the ground. You sweep the area clean with purified mindfulness and concentration. The hindrances don't have a chance. You may even deepen the concentration so much that the mind becomes fixed in a very pleasing calmness. You have cut down all the visible growth – but the roots are still left, very much alive underneath. If you should relax for a moment, new growth springs up again.

There are very decided advantages to control and restraint. Those who practise them with care and dedication find that they live more happily than once was the case. They develop an understanding of the way in which the mind works and this can lead to deep mundane insight, insight into the ways of the world. They develop peace and calmness of outlook, and when the time comes, can look forward to a good rebirth.

The way of control takes much effort to maintain, though. It is hard work and, in the last analysis, all the effort is finally without success. Its results are transient. No amount of this kind of toil can ever produce lasting peace; with the slightest relaxation new hindrances constantly spring up. The roots of the negative aspects of mind are still very much intact. There will be no peace until the roots of suffering are dug out and destroyed.

☆ ☆ ☆

Let us say that, by dint of much trial and error and with a great deal of careful, systematic attention, you have reached purity of mind. You have managed to allay the hindrances so that, for the most part, they are no longer a problem. What do you do now? How do you apply yourself to the meditation practice to get the best out of it at this stage?

It is here that many meditators run into their second major difficulty. The first difficulty lay in discovering the habitual nature of the hindrances. The second is of a different order: it lies in discovering the exact nature of the true path, thus to avoid going astray.

The second major obstacle to the meditation is the belief that it is necessary to create some special state for progress to be assured. The meditator enmeshed in this problem gets attached to various mental factors that arise as the hindrances recede, or believes that it is necessary to develop extremely deep states of concentration before he or she can really progress.

This obstacle, like any other, can take a long or a short time to overcome. Sometimes, the meditator quickly comes to see that such attachments cannot be the correct path to the total elimination of suffering. On other occasions, nothing short of complete experience of all the different states of concentration is going to prove to him that these are not what he is seeking. In the latter case, the detour could take a lifetime or two.

The right path is simply to observe whatever is present, pleasant and unpleasant alike, with unbiased attention. The right path is to observe that all phenomena whatsoever are transient. It is **this** that begins to undermine your reliance on false goals. It is this that begins to undo the misunderstanding that has dogged your mental footsteps for so very long.

The one special meditation that begins to break down the walls of our wrong beliefs is the meditation on transience. It is to pay attention specifically to the rise and fall of things. This is insight meditation. It investigates everything that comes before the eye of attention and notes clearly that it does not last. Nothing lasts. Everything dies. Everything rises and falls.

As the meditation progresses, the impermanent nature of everything becomes increasingly clear. With this growing insight comes the realisation that not only is everything impermanent but also everything depends for its existence on something else; it is conditioned. The Buddha economically expressed this fundamental truth, saying, 'This being, that arises. This ceasing, that ceases.' If that seems too cryptic, consider these examples.

It is impossible to experience feeling of any sort without first there being some kind of physical or mental contact with an object. It is impossible to experience craving unless there is first a feeling or perception, pleasant or unpleasant, that you wish to prolong or get rid of. Further, it is impossible to experience suffering unless there is craving at the root of it. In short, we begin to see that everything is conditioned by something else, everything depends upon something else. Nothing stands alone, unsupported or independent. This is the mark of non-self or *anattā*.

What is the one thing that we all at one time think stands alone? It is the ego, the self. We believe it to be a separate and independent something that never changes, no matter what happens to us and what goes on around us. As the insight meditation practice progresses, this notion of independence is severely challenged. We begin to suspect that the truth about the 'self' is different from that which we had originally supposed. No matter where we look or how hard we try to find something lasting in mind and body, we find only transient phenomena, every one of which is dependent for its existence on other things. We begin to discover for ourselves, through direct experience, that all (relative) things are conditioned. With this discovery, the belief in the existence of a permanent self is weakened; it thins out and begins to fade away.

The perfect meditator resists the allure of the more deeply concentrated and peaceful states of mind. As he or she continues systematically to pay attention to everything that comes before the eye of attention, a deeper understanding of reality begins to emerge. The nature of things seems to change. They become less substantial, less concrete than they seemed before. It begins to look as though the whole process of life goes on by itself without the need for control and management by anyone. The normal idea of a self is seen to be woefully inadequate. There seems no necessity for the existence of a self to govern the business of living. Our long-held assumption about our own importance is discovered to be unwarranted.

For some meditators the experience is quite unnerving at first and they wonder if they are doing the meditation correctly. They are. There is in truth no controlling self to be found, although the meditation must develop further before this is seen as a certainty. After this experience there is often a period of reflection, with the mind much given to thinking of this and that pleasure and ambition. No longer do pleasant things seem so pleasant. No longer do the habitual, escapist fantasies please the mind in the way they once did. The realisation grows that all life truly is *dukkha* and the mark of suffering stands out more and more clearly. This insight into the true nature of life's experiences engenders an intense longing for an escape from the whole sorry mess of *samsāra*. It brings about an intense desire for the bliss of liberation.

Such a strong longing for release prompts reflection on the

reasons why it seems unattainable in spite of his best efforts. The meditator realises that he has not entirely let go of the hindrances; he has been covertly controlling the meditation by picking and choosing which object to observe. Realising that this approach, no matter how subtle now, is in essence no different from what he has always done, he determines to do it properly once and for all and begins consciously to restrain even the subtlest urge to control the meditation. He tries to be aware, without prejudice, of whatever presents itself.

Usually, this is difficult. There arise many aches and pains and not a little despair until the trick is learned. The trick, which is not really a trick at all, is to rest content with whatever appears before the eye of attention; to simply catalogue it along with all the other phenomena that come and go. It is necessary to recognise and label such things as desire for progress and the feelings of helplessness and despair that arise from time to time. Also, one has to identify things like confusion and lack of mindfulness without doing anything about them; to try to change them would be to slip back into the old ways of control and manipulation. This overcomes the conditioned behaviour patterns, the habits, which have dogged one's footsteps for aeons.

Although the long journey to this point has revealed that there is nothing that can be properly called a self, the knowledge is still tender and speculative. It needs strengthening if it is to shatter the fetter[1] of belief that the body is the self.

Careful attention to the rise and fall of things now continues in a way quite different than before. Now there is complete equanimity about the painful and the pleasant things that happen in the practice. No longer is there any extreme reaction to pain and discomfort. No longer is there any elated excitement or attachment to the more pleasing manifestations of the meditation. There is no neurotic urgency to make progress at all costs. Instead, there is a balance of mind that is virtually unshakeable. This balance allows the meditator to observe in a most subtle way and, in due course, he begins to see clearly the

---

[1] Fetter: one of the ten that bind beings to the round of birth and death. They are (i) belief that the body is the self; (ii) adherence to rule and ritual; (iii) sceptical doubt; (iv) sensuous craving; (v) ill-will; (vi) craving for fine-material existence; (vii) craving for non-material existence; (viii) conceit; (ix) restlessness; (x) ignorance. See Chapter 15, page 174.

three marks of all conditioned phenomena: *anicca*, *dukkha* and *anattā*.

One of these three marks becomes exceedingly clear to him. The meditator sees, through direct experience, that his entire universe is transient, not just because everything dies at the end of its lifespan, but because nothing lasts for more than a split second. There really is no duration to speak of.

He may be more attuned to the mark of *dukkha* or unsatisfactoriness. If so, he sees and understands that even the most sublime states, while unquestionably blissful from a relative point of view, are woefully inadequate to ease the ache of constant dissatisfaction.

Perhaps the meditator perceives clearly the mark of *anattā* or non-self. It becomes totally clear that there is nothing that could ever be called 'self'. There is nothing that can be owned. There is nothing that is independent of other things for all things are seen to be irrevocably interlinked. The meditator understands that it is not possible to extract a particular thing from reality, be it self or anything else, and call it a discrete and separate object. Any sceptical doubt he might have experienced about the Teaching is now completely dispelled.

Unbiased observation negates the power of habit. It negates the ignorance that is the bedrock of *saṃsāra*. Removing ignorance in this way means that the mind wakes up. It stops constantly sleeping or escaping into fantasies of its own creation. For the first time the fetters that have bound it so firmly to the false and mundane world have been broken. The journey is well and truly begun.

Having glimpsed the absence of ignorance, craving and hatred clearly for the first time, there can never be any turning back; the meditator is certain of final success. He or she needs a maximum of seven more lifetimes before reaching the end of the road, even if no more meditative work is done in this life. If he does choose to work, however, it may well be that he can finish the job in this very lifetime and become truly free from all suffering. That is the goal of the meditative way, nothing less.

☆ ☆ ☆

It is a great shame when people get sidetracked or misled by their own attachments and habit patterns. The path, once you discover how to walk it, is not so very complicated. The big problem lies in finding directions to it in the first place, and then in translating those directions into practical instructions for the journey.

People tend to forget that there is a time limit on the attempt to find the true path. They think that they have forever to play with. In one sense that is of course true: *samsāra* is endless. You can go round a vicious circle an infinite number of times and still be able to go round again. When it comes to correct directions and skilled guidance, however, these two things are not so endlessly available. The route-maps decay over the centuries, over the lifetimes, whatever may be done to preserve them. Skilled teachers live but a few brief years and then go the way of all flesh. Truly there is not much time for a seeker to establish himself in the right path before the chance is lost, perhaps for a very long time.

If the chance is taken and made the most of, then a meditator can reach the stage of practice called stream-winning. At this point there is no more need to worry about finding the true Teaching or the true path in the future, for both have already been found. Through correct effort the path has been established internally; it is a part of the very makeup of the individual. It is now simply a matter of time before the end of suffering is reached. A stream-winner experiences complete certainty that he **will** come to know the unknown, that the process is unstoppable, no matter what happens.

☆ ☆ ☆

Power is always wielded to allay personal aggravation and distress; the quest for power is ultimately the quest for the complete eradication of dissatisfaction. In the mundane world, however, powerful people can never really find what they seek, for any desired state they manage to establish always turns out to be ephemeral and insubstantial. Such trivial power is not worth much.

To become truly powerful we need to discover how to get what we want all the time. What does anyone want? Freedom from suffering. To be truly powerful is to gain the ability to eliminate suffering totally.

Firstly a meditator gains power over his personal behaviour. With the calmness of mind that this brings, he is able gradually to gain power over the hindrances. As his skills develop he becomes able to perceive the transience of all conditioned things and to pierce the veil hiding reality. Ultimately, he gains power over the arch-enemy, suffering. Removing the causes of dissatisfaction – craving, hatred and, fundamentally, ignorance – he makes an ending of all distress whatsoever. He brings to a successful conclusion the quest for personal power.

11

LOVING-KINDNESS MEDITATION

The development of a mind full of love and friendliness is a very powerful meditation practice. In Buddhist training, there are four 'divine abidings' (*brahma-vihāra*) specifically aimed at developing positive mental attitudes towards all beings, including oneself. They are the divine abidings of loving-kindness (*mettā*), compassion (*karunā*), sympathetic joy (*muditā*) and equanimity (*upekkhā*). These four provide the meditator with a love of others; with the wish to ease their suffering; with the capacity to rejoice in their success; and with the ability, when necessary, to remain cool and self-possessed even under the most appalling circumstances.

Broadly speaking, all are developed in a similar way, with the exception that equanimity is best developed only after some success with the first three, or cold indifference can result.

The practice of loving-kindness begins with a recollection of the dangers and disadvantages of anger and resentment. This is followed by thought given to the major advantages to be gained from loving-kindness itself. Traditionally, these are eleven in number and include sleeping well and waking happily, having no bad dreams, being loved by human and non-human beings, being able to concentrate the mind easily and, not least, the assurance of a fortunate rebirth.

Having outlined the benefits, you then attempt to develop a feeling of friendliness, first towards **yourself** and then to a respected person of your acquaintance. Following that, you move on to develop a loving feeling towards a dearly loved friend, then towards someone about whom you are initially indifferent, and finally towards one you regard as an enemy. The objective of the meditation is to break down the barriers of mistrust and hatred that exist between beings.

The Buddha said, in the famous Parable of the Saw, 'As low-down thieves might carve one limb from limb with a two-handled saw, yet even then whoever should allow hatred to arise and possess his mind, he, for this reason, is not one who practises my Teaching.' Hatred, whether cold dislike or passionate, red rage, is completely to be put aside at will by the full development of loving-kindness.

Why should you develop loving-kindness towards yourself first? The practice of loving-kindness is like *dāna* (giving, generosity) on the mental level; to give something you have to have it in the first place. You have to have that friendly feeling towards yourself before you can wish it for others. If you are trying to generate friendly feelings towards other people then you have no option but to do that through your mind. If your mind is contaminated by negative thinking, then the feeling you generate – your 'gift' to others – is going to be likewise contaminated.

You have to clean out from the mind every least bit of ill-will, agitation, aggression – and sensuality – before the practice of loving-kindness is possible. This requires getting a very strong sense of loving-kindness towards yourself first before it is possible properly to develop it towards other people.

You may find this requirement proves to be a difficulty, initially. For example, you may think you are not a very likeable person, and that there is nothing in your makeup to love, to be friendly towards. Perhaps you see predominantly negative, black states of mind and are secretly convinced that the world would be a better place without you in it. Far from loving yourself, you want forcibly to erase the negative aspects of your character. You want to smash them out, get rid of them, crush them down. In other words you have ill-will towards or hatred of your own negative characteristics.

Such ill-will has to be eradicated – temporarily – before it is possible to do loving-kindness. This means you have to generate at the very least a large amount of tolerance for your own faults and failings, and at the best a recognition that although there may well be faults, any recollection of them has to be put aside for the practice of loving-kindness. You have also to recognise that you are in no way going to get rid of ill-will by having ill-will towards it. That just makes it 'ill-will squared'. It leads to a truly vicious circle where the hatred of the hatred increases the hatred you hate.

If you hate the hatred that you find in your mind, then the action of further hatred merely exacerbates the entire problem. The solution, curiously enough, is to love the hatred you find in your own mind. Perhaps if I were to say, **accept** the hatred you find in your own mind, then it would be a little more palatable. You have to accept the fact of your humanity before you can conceivably generate loving-kindness. You have to accept that human beings – including yourself – are frail creatures, full of all kinds of faults and ugly little characteristics. You are no different from anybody else, and there is nothing particularly to be alarmed about, because all negativity can be overcome, transcended, rendered inoperative, at least for the time being.

If you think about it, self-hatred is really quite conceited. It is to say, 'I should be better than I am, I should be better than anybody else.' There is a constant comparison going on, based entirely on selfish views, based entirely on conceit.

We need to work with a mind that is completely clean, pure and free from taint before it is possible to broadcast anything positive towards another. Not that it is going to be like that all the time, you understand, but it is definitely possible to attain freedom from ill-will and stain on a temporary basis. There are several tried and tested methods for the temporary elimination of hatred, more of which later.

☆ ☆ ☆

Some ask whether one is interacting with the other person in any way when practising loving-kindness meditation. This is quite a difficult question in some respects. Firstly, what is real? You can rightly say that anything you can imagine is real at its own level. The reality of the world you believe to exist around you is simply a belief in the reality of your own ideas. So are the ideas the world? In one sense, of course they are – they are your internal world. But are the ideas what is really out there? Obviously not.

If you are practising loving-kindness, you are trying to develop love for beings in your own mind, for beings as you imagine them to be. To that extent you are practising *mettā* towards 'the world', but the world as seen through your eyes, your concepts. On that basis you might deduce that it will have little or no effect outside.

Having said that, at the conventional level beings do exist –

there is you, there is me, there are other people. There is such a thing as communication between beings both on a physical/verbal level and on a mental level. If you generate thoughts of any kind towards another being, human or otherwise, those thoughts find their mark; they go to that being wherever he or she (or it) may be. The thoughts may have an immediate effect, or they may not.

Some interesting experiments have been performed, in Russia in particular, to test the reality of thought transference. Two individuals are seated in rooms thousands of miles apart and wired up to various physiological testing devices. One person attempts to transmit a mental message or picture to the other. It has been found that they can unquestionably do so, often with startling success. Interestingly, the first indication that it is working is not so much conscious recognition by the recipient but a change in his physiological signs (his blood pressure goes up, for instance) at the exact moment when the other is projecting the thought.

Broadcasting thoughts to other beings unquestionably has an effect on them, with several provisos. You can do all the loving-kindness you like towards an individual but if he is not in a receptive frame of mind, it will have no effect at that time. However, loving-kindness – or any other mental projection – **will** eventually find its mark.

If someone is utterly depressed, you can be as pleasant as you like to him but it does not get through. Later, free from the depressed state, he may feel very warm towards you, being then able to register your actions of perhaps a week or even weeks before. Loving-kindness works similarly: it finds its mark, it has the desired effect, but not necessarily at the precise time it is practised.

Some say that positive thinking directed towards another lodges in the aura of the recipient and rests there until he or she can receive it. Negative thinking does the same thing, not affecting someone who is free from negativity, but finding its mark when negative states predominate.

The practice of the divine abidings most definitely does greatly affect other beings. The generation of loving-kindness is an extremely powerful and positive practice that does nothing but good. Practising friendliness towards the beings in your own mind, you reduce your resistance and irritability with respect to

all beings, human and otherwise. When you meet an individual face to face there is no tension or antagonism, and any interaction is extremely harmonious. To that extent the world is a happier place.

Not only that, but your mind becomes softer and more pliant at all other times. Things aggravate you less; you find the environment less stressful than before. This being so, concentration arises more readily than in a mind untrained in the ways of loving-kindness. For this reason, loving-kindness is a wonderful foundation for the practice of many different kinds of meditation.

The 'far enemy'[1] of the practice of loving-kindness is ill-will or hatred and resentment. It shows itself in various ways, but typically in a feeling of irritation or annoyance with the individual towards whom you are attempting to project friendly, loving thoughts. Some meditators conclude that maybe it would be better if they did not continue to think about such a person, given that negativity constantly arises. The practice should not be abandoned, however.

There are twelve standard techniques for overcoming hatred. One is to go back to an earlier stage in the meditation where you successfully generated a strong feeling of loving-kindness. With this success in mind, you then try again with the individual with whom you are having problems. If repeated attempts fail through irritability or negativity, then you need to investigate the other ways of eliminating hatred. They include finding and concentrating on the other's good points; reflecting on the fact that your own resentment will cause harm **to you**; reviewing the positive and excellent qualities of the Buddha as an example; reviewing the advantages of the practice of loving-kindness; analysing the other being into elements or constituent parts; and giving a gift to the person towards whom you feel so much resentment.

I was speaking the other day to someone who claims to have a vicious hate streak and to be very critical of others. I said, 'I bet without even stopping to think you can name four negative qualities of everybody you know.' He replied, 'No trouble at all!'

---

[1] Far enemy: each of the divine abidings has a near and a far enemy hindering its development. The near enemy is a state of mind similar in tone to the divine abiding, but inefficient. The far enemy is opposite in tone and also inefficient.

I said, 'That is to practise the demonic abiding of hatred and can only lead to harm for you and others. You would be far better off to put the same amount of energy into thinking of four positive qualities for everybody you know. It is going to take much care and attention initially, but the results will be incomparable. Instead of suspicion, depression and resentment, you will generate love, happiness and joy in living – all for the same amount of effort.'

☆ ☆ ☆

For people who are dedicated to the quest for the cessation of suffering, to harm or kill another being deliberately is a complete rejection of that quest. The most valuable thing to any being is its life. Anyone deliberately inflicting death or harm on another being is at that time far from the path to the eradication of suffering.

Consider. In actuality, the universe is love. You could say that it is loving-kindness, although it is more comprehensive than that. It is right and proper, therefore, to trust in the benevolence of the universe; you can safely trust in life itself. Deliberate damage or death at the hands of another temporarily breaks that trust, damages the victim's trust in life, and turns him away from a true perception of reality, away from freedom, away from the spiritual life.

A most significant thing, apparently, about people who have been executed, no matter how 'justly', is the fact that they are appalled at being forcibly divorced from the human race in that way. The true punishment is rejection by their fellows, not death itself. Such rejection can create tremendous psychological damage and it is most difficult for such people to place trust in others again. The sense that the universe is benevolent is entirely swamped and it takes a long time for that trauma to fade.

If, on the other hand, you do withhold damage or death from another, in whatever circumstances, by whatever means, it reinforces their trust and encourages a true perception that life is love. To withhold damage, to withhold death, to stay your hand, to restrain yourself from killing or harming, is an extremely positive move; it encourages people to regard the universe in a positive light. It reinforces their trust in life and in human nature, reinforces their trust that there is good in the world and that there is something worth working towards.

It is impossible to transcend hatred by further hatred. You have either to re-establish loving-kindness for another being with whom your meditation has been successful, or you have to consider other effective means of removing hatred. To succeed at the practice of loving-kindness is impossible unless you eliminate hatred temporarily.

The practice of loving-kindness also helps greatly in overcoming sensual desire, its near enemy, and makes the task of overcoming the other hindrances much easier. With hindrances overcome, there is peace, here and now. The mind is much more settled, much more tranquil and rested than ever was the case before. At times joy arises spontaneously, and the mind is altogether more vibrant, more exuberant and alert. Such tranquillity and happiness rest upon the foundation of self-restraint developed initially by keeping the precepts and enhanced through guarding the senses. Self-restraint gradually evolves into the capacity to suppress the hindrances so that the mind is clean and pure, often for considerable stretches of time.

You can perfect concentration to the level of the jhanas by developing the brahma-viharas, specifically the first three, though most people start, sensibly, with loving-kindness. If concentration developed from the divine abidings is perfected then you live more happily, freer from hatred and other negative states of mind. If you are free from negative states of mind, **any** meditation you do will be far less likely to be interrupted by hindrances. It will be more effective and will stand a better chance of allowing you to develop the insight that leads towards enlightenment.

Concentration itself, including the divine abidings, can only take you just so far, though. It too can be an obstacle to the practice of insight meditation. While it can bring great joy and great peace here and now, it has not tackled the roots of dissatisfaction, disaffection, confusion, craving and hatred upon which suffering rests. Clinging to the peace and calm developed through the practice of concentration is just as much an obstacle as is sensual desire in the first place.

To eradicate the 'roots'[2] (*mūla*) of suffering we have to go to a

---

[2] Roots: three negative and three positive. These are mental proclivities that form the basis for volitional behaviour. They are founded on ignorance of the transient, unsatisfactory and non-self nature of all conditioned things. The three negative roots are craving, hatred and confusion; the three positive, faith, intelligence and speculation.

more subtle level than that accessible by concentration alone. Having developed a basic minimum level of concentration, we then need to employ attentiveness or awareness; we need to pay scrupulous attention to whatever comes before the mind's eye. Concentration allows the mind to focus on one thing or one process without interference from all the clutter and confusion we otherwise find in the mind. Awareness allows the potential to see things never seen before. We need to be able to focus the attention clearly, cleanly and with precision – and then to let it be – if we are to come to the next step.

The next step in the meditative process is the development of insight into the true nature of mind and body. It is the reason for all the careful behavioural and mental preparation that has brought the meditator to this point. The prior work has produced the subtlety of mind necessary to succeed at the task of meditation.

12

SELF-DEVELOPMENT

A human being who indulges gross cravings and hatreds runs the risk of being reborn as a hungry ghost (*peta*) in his next life. A hungry ghost is a being who is trapped in a state of clinging to something that should have been let go long since. Reborn in the realm of the petas, he or she now suffers almost indescribable torments of unsatisfied craving. In the Pali Canon such beings are described in graphic detail. One gluttonous individual was reborn in the peta realm with 'a belly the size of a mountain' that he was forever trying to fill through 'a mouth the size of a pinhole'.

There are those, human and otherwise, who act as helpers and guides to hungry ghosts, trying to get them to see the error of their ways. I read recently about a hungry ghost who had been an entrepreneur. Determined to become rich, he had spent most of his life in that endeavour. By the age of thirty-five, he had amassed a great fortune, though at the cost of his health. Falling ill, his vitality declined so far that he died, though he did not know it. You might ask, how can you not know it? Yet as far as he was concerned, he had become extremely ill and then, quite mysteriously, got better.

Living in his palatial house, he enjoyed all the fruits of his riches. He was puzzled how things happened – meals appeared when no one was there to prepare or serve them, for instance – but he could not make himself worry about it.

The helper in this case, a Cypriot mystic, said that he would regularly go to see this man, now reborn as a hungry ghost, in his self-created prison. He would try to reason with him, telling him that the food only appeared because he created it by mind, telling him that it was not just one or two days he had been there (as he thought) but eighty years. Time moves very differently on that other level: it seems as though one day for a hungry ghost is perhaps as much as fifty or sixty years of humankind's time. The ghost needed to move on but was so attached to his wealth that he could not let it go. That story was never resolved; many others are.

It need not be wealth to which you are attached, of course: you can get attached to almost anything. You can get attached to family, not moving on because you want to ensure that they are well, keeping tabs on everybody. You might be attached to a particular location or a house, or you might get attached to something like drink or bodily pleasures.

We are all beings of love and light, but that light is often obscured by the darkness of ignorance, craving, hatred and confusion. Self-development means to deal with those stains, ultimately to eradicate them completely. It means to get rid of them so they never return. Self-development is to remove the darkness of ignorant attachment, the cause of suffering, to allow the truth to shine through all aspects of our lives.

There are many different paths leading to this freedom but every one of them rests upon the gradual and systematic eradication of self-importance. We have the paradox that self-development means to become less self-important. Self-importance, a sure sign of attachment to ego-gratification, is the very thing that has to go.

Many non-Buddhist ways have postulated higher and lower selves. The higher self is usually taken to be that part of man that is identical with the absolute. It is said to be this 'self' which we have to realise, and the so-called lower self, the egotistical one, that we have to overcome.

When speaking in conventional terms, the Buddha often spoke of self. He said, for example, 'By the self train the self.' He said, 'By the self is evil done; by the self is evil left undone.' Moreover, he said that each of us has not just one but three selves, which I will come to shortly.

Of course the Buddha also taught at the ultimate level that there is no permanent ego-entity, no self, in any of the relative worlds; nor is there such an entity within the absolute. He taught that it is precisely the wrong views and subsequent attachments associated with self that have to be overcome before enlightenment, the end of all suffering, is possible.

All effective ways to freedom offer means to combat the major enemy to the spiritual path: self-importance, conceit, egocentricity. In some, notably the Christian ones, aspirants follow a life of poverty, chastity and obedience. Some Hindu systems urge spiritual seekers to develop *bhakti*, the power of devotion, or *dharma*, devotion to duty and the acceptance of one's lot in this life. In others, rigorous self-discipline is the starting-point. Yet other ways devote themselves to service through such things as teaching or caring for the sick and the dying. All effective ways also employ prayer or meditation as an integral part of their practice.

Always the object is to reduce in importance the scope and intensity of your own wants and needs. One way of doing this is by putting others' welfare ahead of your own: it reduces self-importance. In this, Buddhism is no different and includes some of the finest skilful means for radically reducing that very self-importance.

☆ ☆ ☆

So what about these three selves? The Buddha taught, in common with other ways, that man has three bodies or selves: a physical-body self, a mental-body self and a consciousness self. None of these is a permanent ego-entity, nor is it the absolute, but all need to be trained, developed, for the fullest possible self-development. Very roughly, these three align with *sīla*, *samādhi* and *paññā*, the three major divisions of the noble eightfold path. We will look at how self-development occurs for each of these three selves, at how we can work to reduce self-importance in each of them.

The physical-body self is the being within the gross material sphere, our normal world, our normal everyday self. It is the body – and the mind that is associated with it – whether it is in good health, or sick or damaged. The physical-body self includes the things that body self believes it owns, its environment of things and places. Development for this self includes improving relationships with other people and with all things physical, whether personal or external. It includes the way you look after yourself, your own body, and how you treat others. Let us look at that in more detail.

Personal well-being on the physical level is primarily a matter of health gained from adequate food, shelter and reasonable hygiene. On the other hand personal health is also a matter of restraining excessive indulgence. Overdoing anything – eating, drinking, sleeping or even working – weakens the mind and body by way of stresses and anxieties of various kinds.

For example, gross overeating produces a body that is extremely fat and difficult to move around. Obesity puts an enormous strain on the circulation, the breathing processes, the joints and ligaments and other bodily functions. To drink to excess has disadvantages ranging from physical disease to mental instability, not to mention loss of reputation and livelihood. Excessive sleep is another indulgence, less severe it would seem than drink, but it turns one into something of a vegetable, always seeking unconsciousness, which is hardly the best situation for the successful development of all things to do with the physical body.

The Greeks maintained that to have a sound mind you need a sound body. The Buddha too recognised through his own experience that excesses, even in ascetic practice, damage the body and so make the mind incapable of effective meditation. There was a period when he reportedly lived on one grain of rice a day; clearly not enough to sustain life. He found the flesh falling off so quickly that when he took hold of the skin of his stomach he found that he was holding his backbone. I guess you cannot go much further than that. Such starvation, if prolonged, weakens the mind as well, for mind is dependent on the physical body.

In another period the Buddha tried altering his breathing, trying to force control upon his body by stopping his breathing for as long as he could. His ears began to sing, he got shooting pains through his head and shooting pains through his stomach. Still he held his breath. He reported, 'Mindfulness was established thereby,' – I bet it was! – 'but the body was not calmed.' Through such experience he discovered that he could go no further in developing understanding until the body was calm. Although he had forced the development of great mindfulness, the accompanying extreme agitation precluded any further progress.

In the end he abandoned the extreme ascetic practices as useless for true self-development. He classified them, instead, as self-mortification.

Personal well-being also depends upon the way in which we relate to other people. Reducing self-importance when relating to others is largely a matter of restraining selfish physical behaviour: killing, stealing, wrongful sexual behaviour, harmful talk and intoxication. Such restraint of selfish activity through the five precepts brings about a state of relative calmness in mind and in body and thus eliminates 'the five guilty dreads'.

What are these guilty dreads? This evocative term describes dread arising from misbehaviour. The five arise from breaking the precepts and the consequent fear and anxiety about being found out. It is easy to see how that might apply to killing, to stealing and to wrongful sexual behaviour, for the majority of us are well aware of the dangers involved. Moreover, 'getting away with it' does not eliminate the burden of guilt, however much an offender may like to think that it does. His or her mind is still troubled with a 'guilty conscience' even to the end of a lifetime.

As an aside, I saw recently that forensic science had solved an eight-year-old murder. This success came from careful reconstruction of facial features from the skull of the victim by determining how muscles had been attached and how much flesh there had been overlaying the bones. Once the victim had been identified, the case was quickly brought to a conclusion. I am sure the murderer must have hoped that he had got away with it after eight years, and I am equally sure that he suffered from guilty dread for all that time. It is usually a great relief for wrongdoing to be discovered, for then one can relax, knowing that there is no longer a need to hide one's guilt. Herein lies the wisdom of the confessional: confession cleanses the mind and renders it calm once more.

To steal is nearly always to be in danger of being found out. Even if not, the action will still prey on the mind. Some years ago I heard of a woman in her eighties who sent three pence to a London bus company. As a young girl she had dodged paying her fare and wished to set the record straight before she died; she was uneasy in mind. It is exactly that unease, that dreadful anxiety, that is guilty dread.

Sexual misbehaviour courts disaster in the same way. Activities like adultery carry with them much guilt and fear of discovery. Those committing sexual offences find their minds ill at ease with the result that effective meditation is an impossibility.

Many do not consider indulging in harmful speech and intoxication to be as important as breaking the first three precepts, for all that libel or slander are serious matters in law and continual drunkenness or drug-taking bring personal ruin.

Most of us find restraint of wrong speech very difficult at times and many of us are unaware that its habitual use carries a definite penalty. Wrong speech is to indulge in harsh or abusive language, slander, telling tales or exposing others' weaknesses, defamatory speech and the spreading of gossip and rumour. Such activities unquestionably give rise to guilty dread. If you tear other people's reputations to bits, you inevitably develop a fear of people doing the same to you. That guilty dread, like all the others, is an extremely unpleasant companion and renders the mind unfit for meditation.

Intoxication has a slightly different guilty dread associated with it. You begin to develop deep anxiety about your personal reputation. From wondering what you actually did get up to the night before, you go on to develop more serious concerns. The habitual drunkard fears that he may lose control completely and perform all kinds of degrading actions. He fears for his job, his friends, his marriage. He may even fear losing his hold on reality altogether.

I used to know a man who was well on the way to becoming an alcoholic. His driving licence had been taken away twice but he was still driving a car, even though disqualified. Visiting his local public house, he had drunk an almost unbelievable amount, or so he said. At first I thought he had to be exaggerating, but as the story unfolded, it seemed it had to be true. He had passed out and, on regaining consciousness, could not remember anything and did not know where he was. His neck was bent sharply to one side and he was completely unable to find any purchase with his feet. After struggling for a few minutes he realised why. He was standing upside down on his shoulders against the wall in the cloakroom; he had fallen, and not knowing which way was up, had manoeuvred his legs into the air trying to right himself. After that he got in the car and drove home. Constantly in fear of being caught driving by the police, his family life and his marriage under dire threat from his behaviour, his life was a hell of guilty dread.

Guilty dreads can be allayed by restraining selfish activity. Such restraint also makes you very much safer to be around; it is a very real way of caring for others.

Another aspect of guilty dread is worry about the far future; there is fear of consequences in a future life. Belief in rebirth or an afterlife, and that actions have results, colours your expectations of the future. Performing questionable actions in this life leads to the fear that you might be reborn in unfavourable circumstances in the next.

As you can see, an appreciable amount of self-development can be done on the purely physical level, much of which is to do with restraint.

☆ ☆ ☆

What about the mental body self, though? How does that fit into the picture? With the five guilty dreads banished and a reasonably healthy lifestyle, the way is clear for the development of the mental-body self, the self in the psychic or emotional sphere. This is very much a matter of the control and management of desires and emotions.

Whenever we get what we do not want – pain for instance, we tend to get agitated or depressed. On the other hand, if we succeed in getting something we want very much – calmness in the meditation, perhaps, we may get so elated that we cannot continue. We have to learn the art of balance before we can go on. Depression arises only because we are attached to our own progress; there is great self-importance present. Elation arises for the same reason: there is self-importance underlying the elation; there is a great personal investment in success. Such excessive self-concern needs to be moderated if the meditation is to develop. Buddhist training contains many techniques and practices that help the seeker greatly in this further reduction of self-importance.

As far as the meditation is concerned, emotional development is essential for all meditators once beyond the beginning stages. It is so important that there is a stage on the meditative path called 'overcoming elation and dejection'. If we do not master these two then no further progress is possible.

It works like this. We start meditation enthusiastically. We spend hours, days, weeks and months practising our meditation exercises, studying the books and learning about the Teaching, religiously doing the best we can. The first week or so is probably not too bad – we do not expect to get it all at once, although we would like to. As the weeks go by, though, we may begin to get sorely tried because we are not seeing the kinds of results we want. If we do not adapt ourselves to the reality of the situation, we gradually develop several obnoxious characteristics. We begin to fall into dejection, we begin to get depressed, we begin to get bitter. These make certain that we cannot move on while such self-concern is in evidence.

Sometimes, and it is only sometimes, a meditator gets so distressed while meditating that he gives up in total despair. If that does happen, if he really does give up, then suddenly all problems disappear. The meditation becomes peaceful, still, calm and blissful. The trouble is that you cannot do it by expecting to do it; you really have to let go without any reserve at all. You cannot say, 'I will let go of this pain if I can be sure that I will get calm.' You cannot bargain with it. Letting go is effective only when there are no strings attached.

On the other hand, you may have been working away steadily, doing everything rightly, experiencing no particular problem. As a result, the meditation suddenly goes still and calm, very mindful, very clear. It lasts for about half a second. You are delighted, and there is a tremendous rush of excitement. With the excitement comes agitation so great that it makes it impossible to repeat the experience of peacefulness. The difficulty may last an hour, a day or a week.

Gradually the lessons are learned: until elation is restrained, until dejection is restrained, you are always going to trip up and fall over at that point on the meditative path. Steady progress needs a self-possessed, critical eye; without it, emotional problems are virtually insuperable.

There are definite steps you can take to aid you in this emotional balancing act. It is not just a matter of how you do your meditation moment to moment, the tactics of the meditation; you can undertake specific strategic practices that will help you long term. The four brahma-viharas, divine abidings, are extremely useful in this regard, bringing both emotional balance and sensitivity to the meditator. This is especially true of loving-kindness meditation and compassion.

Loving-kindness is a meditation through which you systematically develop friendliness for yourself and for all beings in the entire universe, in all the three worlds. It overcomes the barriers between people, eradicating fear and generating goodwill, not only in yourself but in those around you. It develops friendliness not only for beings 'out there' but also for the creations of your own mind, including spectres of failure and success.

What does it mean, to overcome the barriers? Imagine you are a passenger in a hijacked aircraft. The hijackers select five people – an old man, a young child, two people in their middle years and you – and say they intend to kill one of you if their demands are not met. The leader insists that you, personally, select the potential victim. Who is it to be? How do you choose? What are your criteria? What would **you** do?

Do you select the old man, since his life is nearly over? Or should it be the child, on the grounds that his life has scarcely begun? Should you do what appears to be the right thing and offer yourself? If you have truly overcome the barriers, the answer is a categorical no, you should not. Any choice at all would indicate partiality: separation and judgement between the worth of individuals. The only right answer is that there is no answer. There is no choice to make, for you see all beings as equal; you see no division. Overcoming the barriers applies not only between human beings but between all beings, on all levels of existence from the so-called lowest to the so-called highest.

Practising loving-kindness meditation generates a stability of mind that is extremely difficult to overthrow. That stability is of great help when it comes to mastering elation and dejection in the meditation practice.

As with all mental developments there are some problems to overcome. The enemies of loving-kindness meditation are sensual desire and ill-will. Sensual desire is known as the near enemy of the practice because it has a similar flavour. Ill-will is the far enemy as it is opposite in intent.

Sensual desire is wanting to see, to touch, to be with the physical individual towards whom you are practising loving-kindness. It emphasises the material body instead of emotional control. In the books there is a story of a man and wife who slept in adjoining rooms. Practising loving-kindness meditation towards his wife, the man 'spent the night fighting against the wall' trying physically to get to her. His meditation was not friendliness in the sense of loving-kindness but its near enemy, sensual desire.

To practise ill-will, the far enemy of loving-kindness, is to practise annoyance and resentment. You might be trying to generate friendly feelings towards someone whom you believe has done you wrong, and before you know it you are thinking,

'Yes, but you know he really did cause me harm, and I don't know that I can ever forgive him.' Off you go, caught up in resentful thinking. Before long you have built a really unpleasant – and damaging – miasma of hatred in the mind. You are practising anger and resentment instead of loving-kindness. It is surprisingly easily done if you are not careful.

Perfect development of loving-kindness meditation demands the restraint of harmful aspects of emotional behaviour, particularly sensual desire and ill-will. With enhanced skill in restraint, the mind is stronger, more concentrated and can sustain insight meditation for longer periods.

To develop compassion (*karunā*), the second divine abiding, is to learn not just to like others but also to wish to help them, to aid them in some fashion. In this meditation, similarly, great care has to be taken to avoid its near and far enemies: self-pity and cruelty.

You can practise compassion in many different ways. It can be done as a pure meditation but it can also be done in a very practical way. One of the most intensely practical is service, and that means physical service, for it is only through physical service that we can engage the emotions and ensure that the exercise does not remain intellectual. Devotion to and care of others both help to develop the mental body by reducing self-importance.

There are countless ways that service can be part of life. It does not have to be something as obvious as running a soup kitchen. For example, the normal activity of bringing up a family demands intense and prolonged service. Compassion in a practical form could be as simple as making a cup of tea for a colleague. It could be caring for the sick, teaching, nurturing the family, either by breadwinning or by cooking and washing. Compassion could be rescuing endangered animals, giving to a beggar – and many, many other things. All these actions can be performed in a spirit of service, where the other person's welfare is put ahead of your own.

Self-pity can be a real enemy in such situations. How many mothers – and fathers – have felt martyred from time to time? They do everything they can for the family, but secretly think, 'They just do not know how much I suffer! Here I go, carrying on day after day, never give a thought to myself!' A strong element of self-pity can creep in and corrupt the service that is compassion, the compassion that is service.

The far enemy of compassion, cruelty, is easier to see. It arises when a worthy action is corrupted by enjoyment in the deliberate infliction of pain. Good intentions have become subverted by stress, overwork, cynicism and bureaucracy. Cruelty of this kind is seen in the schoolmaster who enjoys breaking rulers over little boys' hands. We meet it in the civil servant who is anything but civil. We see it in the nurse who gets perverse pleasure out of giving an injection in the most painful way. Cruelty can creep in through the best intentions, especially if you are overworked, underpaid and life is getting on top of you.

Cruelty as the far enemy of compassion also operates when good works are done from a position of assumed superiority. If you have been in the situation, you will find there is nothing worse than being 'done good to' by someone using you as an exercise to practise charity.

Just as with loving-kindness, the proper development of compassion is a wonderful training and development of emotional control, the self-development of the emotional and mental-body self.

In contrast to simple emotional management, the mental-body self can also be trained through psychic development. Buddha Dhamma contains methods, based on systematic training in concentration and visualisation, that allow meditators to develop awareness and use of the actual mental body. Such an endeavour cannot succeed without skilful emotional control. For example, so-called astral travel, travel in the mental body, needs impeccable emotional management. Without such control the aspiring mental traveller will meet strange situations and react with floods of anxious emotion. This destroys his mental balance, for the time being, and his journey is abruptly terminated by return to the gross physical body.

The capacity to be conscious in the mental body is developed partly by visualisation and partly by the control of emotional responses. This requires a further reduction in self-importance by learning to control and to make little of one's own selfish desires. In this context, imagination can be a tremendous problem.

You are walking alone in the woods at night. How do you respond? Do you see a lurker behind every tree? Or do you never give it a thought? If you are someone who sees shadows come to life with alarming rapidity, then it suggests that your emotional control could use some work. What about having to walk to an isolated car-park when it is dark? How do you react? If you have got a strong imagination that is not controlled, you can have some interesting times. So it is with the person who is attempting to learn how to become conscious in the mental body. If imagination runs away then nothing much can be achieved except fright – or many pleasant but meaningless fantasies.

One way to effective development in the psychic sphere rests upon service to others on a mental level rather than a physical one. Again, loving-kindness meditation and compassion meditation can be used. In this context, one way of practising loving-kindness meditation is to imagine yourself going on a 'walkabout', to visualise yourself going to see the individual towards whom you are intending to practise the loving-kindness. You try to visualise, if not the entire journey, then at least arriving at his or her dwelling place. You then seek them out and try to visualise them in their current environment while developing loving-kindness towards them.

Earlier, I mentioned those who help hungry ghosts by dealing with them face to face. There are other levels of existence where the mental traveller can give aid. One aspect of such work is going out to help at deathbeds. It is said that when a person is dying, very often deceased relatives gather to help that person's transition from one life to the next. Not only do deceased relatives attend the dying: there are also those from this side who are trained helpers. These individuals attend wherever there is a need, such as on a battlefield, or for those who would otherwise die with no one in attendance.

Sometimes when an individual dies suddenly – for example, a soldier in battle, he may not know that he has been killed. If you have ever suffered an accident involving a sharp cut or blow, you will know that it does not hurt at the time; the pain comes later. It may be a severe injury but all you feel is a blow, which might physically move you, might even knock you down, yet you do not realise you have been hurt or damaged until later. If the blow is fatal, you may know it even less, because you pick yourself up, leaving the physical body behind, and wander off in your mental body trying to continue whatever you were doing.

Without understanding what is happening, the newly-dead

individual may wander about in confusion for a considerable time. His acceptance of his new life would be far easier with some knowledge of the facts. It always helps to know what is going on. Wherever possible, there are trained helpers who assist those newly departed to find their mental feet, and point out to them the realities of their situation. These helpers are often learning to develop emotional control, developing the capacity to help others and minimise their own self-importance.

Someone I know spent a week in a cottage in the heart of the country. In doing his nightly walkabout, his loving-kindness meditation, he suddenly found himself grappling with someone wearing a cowled habit. Taken aback, he asked his ghostly assailant what was going on. The cowled man angrily demanded that the intruders, my friend and his wife, should leave 'his' home immediately. The meditator informed this 'hungry ghost' that he was dead, but was met with disbelief. He had to try a different approach.

'What date is it?' he asked. '1760,' the figure replied. 'Have I got news for you!' said the meditator, and told him that it was now 1990. He repeated to the hungry ghost that his physical life had ended and pointed out that he was clinging to a house that was his no longer. My friend instructed the hungry ghost to let it go, to give it up, telling him that he should move on and accept his 'new' condition. In this case, that was all that was needed. The figure disappeared and there was no more disturbance on that or subsequent nights.

The ghost clearly thought it had been a matter of days, for he still believed the date to be 1760, when in fact over two hundred years had passed. It shows how differently time passes on other levels. Because such individuals, such hungry ghosts, have not learned emotional management, have not learned self-development in the mental sphere, they are trapped until someone can assist them.

Gaining control over one's emotional state is essential to full self-development; without it progress beyond the shallows of spiritual experience is not possible. Such control need not include the ability consciously to travel in the mental body to assist others, but it must be skilled enough to restrain elation and depression that otherwise corrupt the meditation practice. Control of the emotions is hard work and, to start with, does not seem very rewarding, for one comes face to face with one's own inadequacies time and again. With perseverance, however, emotional control is always won and the way is then clear for further self-development.

☆ ☆ ☆

What about the consciousness self? This, as its name suggests, is development within the sphere of consciousness itself. It includes awareness of refined, concentrated levels of mind as well as actual recognition through experience of what the Buddha's Teaching labels right view and right thought.

View structure – how you see your world, how things fit together – is particularly important. This is adjusted and corrected by study and experience gained from life itself, whether following this Teaching or not. Experience will show, for example, that stealing leads inexorably to suffering.

Wrong view – such as believing there is no point in ethical action – and wrong thought – assuming that self-gratification is the only measure of success – lead to increasing self-importance and distress. Right view, in contrast, is the idea that actions do have results, that for every unselfish action we reap a positive beneficial resultant and for every inefficient action, every selfish action, we reap suffering. Right view transforms for the better the life of the individual who adopts it; it leads to increasing happiness and contentment.

Right thought is thought free from selfishness, thought free from craving and free from hatred. If you eliminate, even temporarily, craving and hatred, at that time there is no self-importance in the mind. Continued experience brings the realisation that self-importance is craving and hatred; they are synonymous. To develop right thought is to practise the restraint of selfishness. Such restraint leads to extreme peace of mind and what I call mental cleanliness. It leads to a great deal of personal ease and satisfaction.

It is also possible to develop the consciousness self in a really practical way through meditation, through becoming conscious at levels beyond those concerned with materiality. This subject is beyond the scope of this evening's talk so I do not propose to go into detail. Suffice it to say that it is entirely possible to be fully conscious at levels most would call abstract, where the object of consciousness is not material but is space, consciousness itself or perception. Becoming conscious at these levels, one learns that selfishness and grasping operate even here. That, and the restraint that ensues, are aspects of the development of the consciousness self.

There are many advantages to self-development through reducing self-importance. They include: an upwelling of spontaneous joy, where spontaneous loving-kindness fills the mind from time to time; constant acceptance of people and things as they are, without wishing to change them; reduction in the levels of criticism, worry, anxiety and fear in the mind; sound knowledge of right action, of knowing what really helps people, including a knowledge of what really helps yourself. Reduction in self-importance also leads to receiving help from other people spontaneously and often when you least expect it. All these advantages accrue from reducing self-importance.

It does not end there. In addition, there is assurance of a good destiny: you know you will be reborn into better circumstances than previously. You develop a trust in life, feeling that everything works out for the best in the end. You gain an increasing knowledge of *kamma* and *vipāka*, action and result, and a greater freedom to experience life as it is. You experience a reduction in attachment and a consequent reduction in distress. You begin to see that so-called disasters always – and I do mean always – have an unexpected benefit. There is no such thing as something that is wholly bad.

13

THE LIMITS OF PERCEPTION

As part of one's self-development, it is extremely beneficial to learn a system of analysis that goes beyond the personal. The most helpful kind is one that deals with the ultimates of human experience in a way that leads the individual towards the eventual eradication of suffering. Dhamma, the Teaching of the Buddha, includes several systems of analysis developed over his teaching lifetime. Any one of these is effective.

In one, the Buddha analysed the entirety of human experience into five *khandha* or 'groups of grasping': body or materiality, feelings, perceptions, volitional tendencies and consciousness. This evening I want to talk to you about the group of grasping after perceptions.

The Buddha's primary objective was always to show people how they might come to the complete and total eradication of suffering; that was what every word of his Teaching was about. That is what is available to each of us today.

He pointed out that all suffering arises dependent upon a cause. It does not arise without reason. Suffering of any description arises only if there is prior craving for an object. That object might be a mental state, a thing, a person or anything else, and has first to be perceived. Thus the *khandha* of perception, the group of grasping after perceptions, is central to any understanding of the Buddha's Teaching. Dealing as it does with all possible perceptions, past, present and future, it includes everything we have ever wanted or may ever dream about.

The Buddha taught his monks the importance of perceptions in many different ways. Like anyone else, they suffered from sensual desire from time to time. Once, he said to them, 'Imagine that there is far away a village of which you have never heard. In that village there is a beautiful young woman – wonderfully attractive, with long dark hair, big dark eyes and all the things that men dream of. Could you, monks, lust after that particular person?'

They said, 'How could we? We do not know she exists. We do not even know there is a village. How could we desire that particular individual?'

You cannot want something that you do not know about. You cannot desire something you have not perceived or imagined, as the Buddha's example illustrates.

All suffering arises on craving for an object. Unless there is contact through the senses (including the mind) with some kind of object, craving cannot arise and neither can suffering. The object does not have to be real; you need only believe that it is real. Then craving and suffering are possible.

What is real? If all of us agree that there is a mountain, and there is a man called Charles and a woman called Jane, we say those things are real; we say those perceptions are accurate. But when looking at the world, there is always the possibility of error. There are many common mistakes in perception, ranging from, 'Oh, I'm sorry. I thought you were somebody else', to seeing, hearing or sensing things that are not even there.

Once when travelling in a truck across the desert of eastern Afghanistan, very hungry and very tired, I saw a herd of horses gallop across the road in front of us. The driver did not bat an eyelid and drove straight through them. I was horrified, and it was only the lack of impact that proved to me that they were not real. I had definitely seen them – there was no question about it – but they were not there at all.

We are all familiar, I think, with optical illusions. You can see something that is not there at all. Seeing it, you can then want it, fear it, wish to get rid of it.

It happens with the other senses as well. I heard an interesting experiment described on the radio some years ago. Take a pellet of bread a millimetre or two in diameter, cross your index and middle fingers, put the pellet between the tips of them and roll it backwards and forwards on a hard surface. What do you feel? You feel, quite distinctly, two pellets of bread, though you know there is only one. If you have your eyes closed it is very convincing and almost impossible to tell what is real. It is an error of perception based on the sensation of touch.

Everyone has experienced a bad smell that seems to linger. Perhaps something has started to decay in the fridge. You clean it out religiously but you are sure you can smell it for days afterwards. Can you? Is it real? I wonder.

Lots of mistaken perceptions can occur on hearing. At the beginning of my training in London, my meditation was plagued by the sound of ambulance sirens from the road in front of the monastery. This got so bad I just did not know whether I was coming or going. It went on and on and on. It slowly dawned on me that the frequency of the ambulances was excessive; there surely could not be so many. Taking some time off, I sat at the front window and watched the road. No ambulances. Very suspicious, I thought.

Going back to my room, I meditated and observed very carefully whenever I heard a siren. What I discovered was this. There were various odd tones and sounds, electrical hums and buzzes, that formed part of the background noise. Seizing on some of these incidental sounds, I was converting them into an (imaginary) ambulance siren. I had been torturing myself. I had been hating, and getting very resentful about my inability to control, something which did not exist. Without question, most of the ambulance sirens had not been real. I only thought they were. Once I could observe the process clearly, my problem was solved.

Mistaken perceptions involving the five physical senses are fairly obvious, but what about the mind itself? What of something like paranoid delusions, where someone believes he is being persecuted and that there are people out to get him, following him, spying on him? The persecutions he imagines are not real, but the paranoid wholeheartedly believes that they are.

When we try to get rid of or to acquire objects that are not real, we experience tremendous frustration and distress because, clearly, the acquisition, or the getting rid of, is impossible. We need instead to deal with the mistaken perception itself.

Ignore-ance of this fact, ignore-ance of the mistake, and trying to deal with an unreal object as though it were real, leads to mad behaviour. The paranoid thinks his persecutors really do exist, and he takes many and devious steps to avoid them. He knows he is hunted, he knows his tormentors exist, for he sees proof of it all around him, and he takes every measure he can think of to foil them. In a similar way, I wanted to get rid of the ambulance sirens, but they did not exist. I had first to see that they were errors in perception. Only then could I do something about the problem.

Without meditative training, it is no easy task to remove the obvious, coarse kinds of errors in perceptions that deal with the conventional world. In the West, this burden is generally shouldered by psychiatrists who try, through various forms of analysis, to normalise perceptions for their patients. If this is not possible, then the careful use of drugs may help to attenuate the imagination and damp down the emotions, enabling the patient at least to live with the consensus reality, with what everybody else believes to be real.

In the East, there is far less horror of madness. Mad or deviant people are tolerated as long as they do not cause any particular upset in the community. Conforming to the social norm is a question of personal responsibility. It is up to you whether you fit in or not; no one else particularly minds. After all it is your *kamma*, your responsibility, your life. If you choose to be sufficiently mad not to eat, if you choose to be non-conformist to the extent of living in rags on a riverbank when you need not, that is your affair. Madness and deviant behaviour is tolerated in the East in a way quite different from the West.

Non-conformist behaviour is tolerated in part because of what Buddhism calls mundane right view: the (correct) view that every action we perform is our own responsibility. In the East, they have the clear awareness – for the most part – that each individual is responsible for his or her own actions. If you look at the West, that is not necessarily believed. We are more inclined to believe we are responsible for other people's actions but not necessarily for our own, curiously enough.

There are groups who are concerned to police others' behaviour on the grounds that it is unethical or harmful in some way. 'Animal rights' activists have been in the news recently, reportedly committing terrorist-style aggression against those who have displeased them. It seems that they assume their own evil actions to be entirely justified by the good cause they espouse. Further, it is not uncommon for someone defending a criminal charge to claim he was not responsible, due perhaps to the circumstances of his early life!

Mundane right view states that every action produces a result. If you act in a way which is inefficient, which is selfish, which is contrary to common sense in the conventional world, you can expect to suffer painful consequences. You can expect to be ostracised as a direct result of your choice not to conform. Depending on the kind of action, you can expect to be punished by being imprisoned, maybe even executed. If, however, you choose to act in ways that agree with the consensus reality, you restrain extreme selfish urges, find yourself at peace with your fellows and lead a reasonably contented life. Mostly, things go very well.

But even with mundane right view, there are still many hidden errors of perception that lead to craving and distress. To discover these more subtle errors, we have to step outside the convention into a different world. We have to leave behind what most people believe to be real and move into the world of direct experience.

The world of direct experience is a different world entirely. It starts from the premise that a million people believing something to be true does not, on that account, make it a fact. Consensus reality is very often wrong. It is often very wrong. When examined closely, it contains many unwarranted assumptions.

To discover the errors in mundane right view, we have to analyse our perceptions with trained attention. We need to discover the truth of sensory experience. We need to prove what is the basis of perceptions.

In the West philosophers like Kant and Wittgenstein have demonstrated with elegant logic the limits of our certainties; they have produced theoretical proofs of what is really real, of what we can know for a fact. This has not helped them to eliminate or even reduce suffering, because the proofs are theoretical.

In the East, in contrast, wise men have since time immemorial preferred direct experience. They have undertaken rigorous training in meditation to discover at first hand that on which we base our knowledge, the building blocks of mind and matter, as it were. Knowing this directly, they have sought always to penetrate behind even this level of appearance to apprehend what is really real[1].

---

[1] The division into West and East is somewhat arbitrary, for both kinds of approach to truth are found in each part of the globe. In the West, there is the mystic tradition now commonly associated with Christianity, but present in the old religions of the West for thousands of years. This stresses direct experience in the same manner as Oriental teachings, the specifics naturally differing according to custom and culture. In the East, there is a tradition of logical and scientific enquiry going back longer than Western civilisation has existed. For example, the great dynasties of China were responsible for some of the finest philosophies and also the greatest advances in science that the world has ever known.

☆ ☆ ☆

What is really real?

All we can find when we look closely are separate sights, sounds, smells, tastes, touches and mental states, each conditioned by other factors. None of them lasts for more than an instant. At this level of analysis, conventional reality turns out to be false. Only materiality and mentality exist: only the *khandha* of materiality and the four mental *khandha*. At an elementary level, there are only the four great elements of matter and the fifty-two *cetasika* or mental concomitants[2] that define mind. There is no mountain, there is no man called Charles, no woman called Jane. They do not exist, and so perception has changed. At this level, the conventional world is no longer perceived as really real.

Some believe that if you can see through the apparent reality of the conventional world, you must inevitably come to the end of suffering. They believe that all you have to do is to perceive that the world as we know it is in one sense an illusion and the task is finished, the journey ended. This would be to stop short, however. There is considerably more to do.

Consider: what are we left with? We are left with what we could call ultimate reality, a collection of material and mental components that come into and go out of existence with extreme rapidity. But – and here is the difficulty – most meditators tend to see these fleeting mental factors as real entities that can somehow be controlled, developed or eliminated.

Imagine that you wish to analyse in detail the movements of a horse jumping a fence. With a high-speed movie-camera you take many pictures. Playing back at normal speed effectively slows the action so you can analyse easily. You print still photographs, extracting segments of activity that you can examine at leisure.

---

[2] Mental concomitants (*cetasika*): aspects of mind arising with consciousness and comprising ethically wholesome, unwholesome and neutral qualities. For example, faith, mindfulness, fear-of-blame, fear-of-shame and compassion are ethically wholesome or efficient qualities; greed, hatred, delusion, worry, recklessness of ethical consequences and conceit are ethically unwholesome or inefficient; feeling, perception, volition, concentration, energy, interest and intention are neutral as such and take their ethical coloration from the state of consciousness with which they are associated.

You identify each segment as a separate component of the action, as a thing. You say, 'This is the stage where the horse's front legs come off the ground. We will call it "lift-off". Here, the entire horse is airborne. We will call this component of the jump "flight".' You follow it right through, identifying every aspect of the jump.

Out of a beautiful, fluid movement you have created a whole series of component parts or 'things'. You know that they are not permanent, that they are transient, but you define them as the ultimate constituents of 'the jumping experience'.

Perhaps you decide that your analysis is not after all fine enough. You take more pictures at a higher speed still, slowing the action even further. The resulting stills allow you to analyse movements in even more detail. You have created a greater number of stages, more things, a finer degree of resolution.

Is there an end to this process? Practically speaking, I suppose there is, dependent upon camera technology. Theoretically, though, you could go on endlessly, further refining your analysis of the jumping horse.

Do any of the segments you have isolated exist as independent things? Of course not: they are just abstractions. They do not really exist at all. There most certainly is **something** there, of course, but as soon as you analyse it, as soon as you define it in some way, as soon as you put a name to it – with words or pictures – then you have distorted the original experience. You have distorted reality, which has no divisions or components at all; it is seamless.

Many people crave to possess qualities like concentration and wisdom, love and compassion. People, including meditators, hate – and want to destroy – inefficient mental qualities like hatred itself. They wish passionately to eliminate them entirely. Such craving and hatred, such passionate desire, is based on the belief that these qualities like love and compassion, or hatred and greed, can be established permanently. Consequent on this belief arise craving and enormous suffering.

It is a very real problem and needs a very particular solution. Psychiatry cannot remove these subtle errors of perception. Concentration or calming meditation (*samatha*) is no good, either. Loving-kindness meditation (*mettā*) does not help at all, nor does compassion (*karunā*). There is only one way: *vipassanā* meditation, the perception of transience.

The perception of transience is the only way, and it has to be applied to these individual factors, like love and compassion, wisdom, hatred, craving and all other aspects of mind. Perception of transience must be applied, with subtlety, to all the individual factors that go to make up mind and body.

When this is done, it becomes clear that any thing – conventional or ultimate, material or mental, past, present or future – is so transient that it is questionable whether we can say accurately that it exists at all. We find eventually that any perception at all is misleading, is not accurate.

That discovery leads to an interesting realisation. The only things we can crave for or hate are things that do not exist, for there are no real things in the first place, neither conventional nor ultimate. There never were and there never will be. There is only **this** which is not nameable. There is only reality itself. This is the beyond of which the Buddha spoke in his third noble truth. This beyond is beyond the conventional world but also it is beyond the ultimate world; it is beyond mind and body.

The perception of transience utterly purifies the mind of craving and hatred. Knowing by experience – and I do stress it has to be by experience – that there is nothing to crave for, craving becomes an impossibility. It is not that you give up craving for things, it is not a question of restraining it. You find it impossible to crave for anything, anywhere, anytime, for you know that there is literally nothing to crave for. Not people, not places, not even wisdom and compassion.

Why are we so slow to see this truth? We all fear the unknown and cling to the familiar, no matter how false it may be, hoping blindly that things will work out somehow. But sometimes life circumstances drive us to reconsider, to change, to examine, to learn. If you have led a life of selfishness, for example, life will eventually draw your attention to it. If you have lived always trying to satisfy only your own wants and needs, there comes a time, in this life or the next, when you experience mistreatment, abuse and ingratitude in an almost overwhelming way. Your suffering becomes truly intense and desperate, and although it is actually the painful results of past action, it seems as though life itself is forcing you into a position where you need to change. When you recognise the need to change, the resulting search for an answer can lead to the discovery of the path to freedom.

What is life like without errors of perception? That is a

question almost impossible to answer. You could say that life is the same but different – and yet that is not right, for someone who knows the truth about perception is a changed individual. Still as capable – or as incapable – as before of operating and working in the world, he or she is nevertheless decidedly not of that world. He has gone beyond the normal scheme of things, has become one of 'the great ones whose task is complete', to quote the Pali Canon, 'whose burden is laid down, who has no more to do, who is worthy to receive gifts'.

His knowledge is unshakeable. He can never fall back into ignorance, for he sees perfection itself and knows it is everywhere. He has overcome ignorance, craving and hatred, and can never again perform actions leading to rebirth and suffering. He is forever free.

Such people have completed the task of the Buddha's Teaching. They have come to the end of their training. It is entirely possible today just as it was two and a half thousand years ago. There are people alive today who have completed the spiritual search and can show others how to do the same.

This way, this path the Buddha taught, is the most wonderful legacy. Meeting it as you have done, it is well worth making every effort to follow it, trying every day to practise, trying to understand, trying to come for yourselves to that experience that transcends all worlds. There is truly nothing more worthwhile.

14

SIGNPOSTS TO FREEDOM

We recognise things by their distinguishing features, their marks, or their signs. This is particularly important when we come to Buddhism.

I can clearly remember an incident that occurred when I was about eighteen. Walking down a country lane on a perfect day in springtime, I saw cycling towards me a young woman I guessed to be about my own age. She had long blonde hair and wore a bright red skirt contrasting strongly with the new green foliage of the hedgerows. Immediately interested, and full of anticipation, I started searching for something arresting to say. As she drew nearer, though, I realised I had made a mistake: she was not blonde, but grey; not eighteen, but about sixty-eight. I had quite misread the signs that, for me, indicated a young person.

We rely upon such marks and signs more than we know: they are fundamental. When we come to the spiritual search, to the task of transcending the relative world, the recognition of signs or marks becomes particularly important. In Buddha Dhamma, the Teaching of the Buddha, we learn that anything in the relative worlds – the world of desire, the world of form or the formless world – is always recognisable by three specific qualities, marks or signs. Relative things are always transient, always unsatisfactory in some way, and all things are non-self: they do not have a permanent, unchanging 'core' or identity.

The object of the spiritual search, *nibbāna* – the absolute, the beyond, that which is not relative – is in contrast always free from all signs: it is signless.

It is no secret that there are many roads to truth. Just think of the number of religions in the world. They all say different things, however, and this leads to great difficulties between people. Discussion of the merits and demerits of different religious views can get very heated. I remember dire warnings from my youth never to discuss religion or politics with strangers, especially in public houses.

Even when religion is discussed seriously, there can be almost overwhelming problems. Many say, 'Only my way is the right one.' Or, 'My way is the **only** one.' Witness the past conflicts between different sects in Christianity. Let alone 'past conflicts' – there are plenty of present ones. And not only in the Christian world – the world of Islam is in ferment with a movement back to fundamentalist ideas.

In 1974, I was in Thailand for the first time, looking at Buddhist teaching methods in that country. I was surprised to find serious contention and rivalry between different Buddhist teachers, and between the students of different teachers, regarding just what was the 'right way'. There were different meditation systems, different groups, different societies. One, the 'Society of Heavenly Grandfathers', suggested that all our troubles would be over if we could learn to communicate with our ancestors through deep meditation. In this way we could gather the wisdom of those dear departed ancients and apply it to our own lives.

A Burmese monk led another group, and based his instruction on Mahasi Sayadaw's system of *vipassanā*. He taught straight-down-the-line *vipassanā*, no frills, very serious, and definitely critical of 'heavenly grandfathers' and the like. He, quite rightly, believed that it is possible to come to enlightenment in this very lifetime, and taught accordingly.

Another renowned and well-respected Buddhist monk taught that it is impossible to become enlightened today, that all we can do is prepare for the future. He was adamant that to become enlightened, we need the instruction of a living Buddha. Eventually, in the aeonic future, the next Buddha, Metteyya, will be born. Then – and then only – will we be able to realise the goal of the Buddha's Teaching.

Any conflict within Buddhism is at the verbal level: people debate and disagree, sometimes vehemently, but I have never heard or read of it escalating into violence. Buddhist groups go their own ways, aware of one another but not ready to go to war over a difference in approach. When religious conflict becomes extreme, however, it results in real and bloody violence in Crusades, *Jihad* or Holocaust. Admittedly such violence is extreme but religious differences of opinion can get extremely contentious, especially when so many say, 'Only my way is right.'

On the other hand, there are severe problems with trying to be excessively fair-minded. Some maintain that all religious ways are effective – which may to a greater or lesser extent be true – but then make the mistake of trying to align exactly the details of different teachings. Such an approach can lead only to confusion. For example, if one religion believes in a creator god, and another – like Buddhism – does not, how can you possibly align their practices in any meaningful way?

Followers of both theistic and non-theistic teachings do at least have a system, an ordered body of practices to follow. There are those, however, who maintain that any system or method forms a complete barrier to the spiritual quest. On this basis, there are systematic ways, and what I think I must call 'non-system' ways (although that is perhaps a misnomer, as you will see in a moment).

Systematic ways aim to reach the highest perfection of which man is capable by efforts systematically applied both to personal conduct and to prayer or meditation. They include all religions on the planet, great and small, and schools and sects within those religions. For instance, in Buddha Sasana, the Teaching of the Buddha, there are many different sects that form two major schools, namely Theravada and Mahayana. There are different techniques of meditation within those schools and sects, though the goal is the same: the total eradication of suffering and distress.

In contrast, there are the 'non-system' ways. The non-system approach says that as we are essentially perfect already, we have nothing to do – except, of course, to wake up and realise that fact. They say that trying to change ourselves by following any systematic path prevents us from seeing reality as it is. The most famous non-system is probably Zen; the most famous teacher of a non-system, J. Krishnamurti. Zen itself does advocate meditation – the very word *zen* means meditation. It came originally from the Sanskrit *dhyāna* (*jhāna* in Pali). Historically, Buddhism migrated to China, where the word became *ch'an*, and finally to Japan, where it became *zen*. The word simply means meditation.

I do not think that Zen regards meditation as a system, but

other non-system proponents definitely do. They say that
meditation is a system in itself, and that it is therefore harmful to
the spiritual quest.

When highly respected, intelligent and dedicated teachers are
divided by supporting two such radically different views of the
search for truth and understanding, we have to ask ourselves
why. The differences seem impossible to reconcile. Is one side in
the debate completely mistaken – however well-meaning? It
does seem unlikely, given the calibre of the people we are talking
about. They must each be talking about the selfsame thing, the
same realisation. There is, after all, only one absolute. So where
is the problem? Why is there this fundamental disagreement
about the path to the beyond?

All ways (and non-ways, for that matter) aim for the highest.
But there are two types of description of that highest: positive
and negative. Positive descriptions include such things as the
one, perfection, eternal life, freedom, union, the highest
happiness – all signifying some highly positive state towards
which we may wish to aim. These descriptions are unavoidably
inaccurate and freely acknowledged to be so by the very people
who use them.

Although still difficult, a safer method to deal with what lies
beyond description is to use a negative. Those who use negative
descriptions recognise that the absolute possesses no nameable
attributes, whatever people may choose to call it, and try to
avoid labelling it with familiar terms. The beyond is non-dual
(not one, notice, for one implies two); the deathless; the unborn,
unoriginated and unbecome; the end of birth and death; the end
of craving, hatred and delusion; the signless (the opposite of the
relative world with its signs).

But there are still traps within the negative description. To
come to full understanding it is necessary to transcend all
opposites – good and bad, tall and short, near and far, sign and
signless, positive and negative. It is hardly a new problem, of
course. The Buddha, over two and a half thousand years ago,
said, 'You should, through understanding, put away even right
mental objects; how much more must you also put away the
wrong ones.' You have to transcend both good and bad if you
are aiming at enlightenment.

In a famous parable, the Buddha likened Dhamma, his
Teaching, to a raft. He said that having crossed the flood of

samsāra on the raft of Dhamma, the wise man does not carry the raft on his back after he goes ashore: he leaves the raft, the Teaching, behind. Zen, more graphically, says, 'Kill the Buddha.' These admonitions say that to come to enlightenment, you have ultimately to give up your reliance upon the Teaching, and even upon the Buddha himself.

In fact, all systems have to be transcended, in all cases. The path has to be left behind to arrive at your destination – but you cannot do without the path. To update the Parable of the Raft, say you go from here to London on the train. You need the train to get to London, but you do have to get out of the train and leave it behind when you get there.

In contrast, non-system people seem to have a pathological distrust of 'trains'. They prefer, instead, to rely upon 'spontaneously tending' towards their spiritual destination. If, however, you rely upon spontaneously tending towards London and religiously avoid the train – or any organised route, you are extremely unlikely ever to get there. Krishnamurti is on record as saying that in about sixty years of (non-system) teaching, he was not sure if even one person had understood what he was saying.

You need more than an intellectual understanding that systems have to be transcended: you must have the experience.

One student, in his early forties, had come to an impasse in his meditation; he had come to a dead stop. Talking with him, it was evident that his problem centred on his belief that he needed a better education. He had acquired no qualification at all, and had a deep-seated admiration of people with degrees. He believed that he needed to be educated to get any further, and this was holding him up. We agreed that while he could see intellectually that he did not need an education, the problem lay in his emotional conviction that he did. That being so, he should seek further education in the interests of his meditative journey.

He left his job and found a place on a degree course. After about three years of the four-year course he commented, 'You know, this is a waste of time. Education does not give you anything of use in the meditation.' In complete agreement, I pointed out that, now, he knew this for a fact. His meditation deepened dramatically after that.

Intellectually, he had been perfectly able to appreciate that having a degree would not make much difference, but he had yet to know it by experience. Once he had the experience, nothing could hold him back.

That is the difference between intellectual and experiential understanding: an intellectual education gives you nothing but information; personal experience gives you real understanding. You have to go along the path, though the path is not ultimately going to get you there.

The Buddha was perfectly aware of the dilemmas inherent in the problem of system and non-system. He recognised that without a path, without a system to follow, most people would not come to realise the truth. He also knew that any system had to be transcended for enlightenment to occur. So he taught both. He taught the system and he taught its transcendence.

☆ ☆ ☆

The Buddha's system – Dhamma, the Teaching – he summarised wonderfully well in four truths: there is suffering, there is an origin of suffering, there is a cessation of suffering, there is a way leading to the cessation of suffering. That way is the eightfold path. It has eight 'steps' or factors that are most definitely not sequential, as some have claimed. They are: right view, right thought, right speech, right action, right livelihood, right effort, right mindfulness and right concentration. Without the eightfold path it is not possible to travel to your destination.

The eight components are divided into three sections relating to personal discipline, meditation and wisdom. You need to lead a disciplined life, a restrained life; many would call it a moral life. You have to train the mind so that it can observe, so that it can be quiet, so that it too is restrained. You need also to train the mind in understanding. Study is necessary, for you have to learn about the world from a viewpoint different from that most common in the West.

Each of us has to learn that actions have results; that we, alone, are the arbiters of our fate. Our situation right now is the outcome of all the actions we have done in the past. They have moulded us, forced us, guided us, led us into this particular set of circumstances. If we do not like our circumstances, if we find them difficult in some way, then we can change. We can change our lifestyle, our approach to living, our way of doing things, and we can find that life will improve as a direct result.

The foundation of the eightfold path is to accept responsibility for our own condition, and not to say it is the other person's fault. It is to recognise that our circumstances, good and bad, are our own responsibility.

Tied in with the recognition of self-responsibility is Condition Dependent Origination (*paticca-samuppāda*). In addition to showing how suffering arises from lifetime to lifetime, this shows that even the **momentary** arising of distress is conditioned by the way we respond to events in the present. If we respond with craving and hatred, with fear and anger, we experience much more distress than if we respond with openness, love, tolerance, compassion and other similar qualities. It is not just a neat theory: you can actually see it happening. Again we come back to the point that it is not enough to know it intellectually. You have to experience it as well. That is when the real changes for the better come about.

The Buddha, as part of his system, also taught four jhanas – the deeper levels of concentration which lead to great depths of calm and peacefulness. Last but by no means least he taught *vipassanā*, insight meditation. This is essentially the perception of transience, one of the three marks of all conditioned phenomena, and leads to four different 'fruitions'.

Someone attaining the first fruition he called a stream-winner, destined irrevocably for enlightenment after a maximum of seven more lifetimes. The second he called once-returner. The meditator attaining the third fruition is a non-returner: instead of being reborn after death in *kāma-loka*, the world of desire, he is born in the 'pure abodes'[1], there to realise full enlightenment. Last of the four, the *arahant*, or fully enlightened one, has completed the path and has eradicated the roots of suffering.

Vipassanā, the system of meditation we practise here, examines all we know. Using *vipassanā*, we conduct a personal search for the highest in everything we can describe or recognise. We look at all aspects of body, feelings, mental states and specific mental qualities – always searching for perfection. We examine each and every aspect of mind and body to see if it holds the secret we are looking for.

Systematic examination proves – by experience – that everything relative is without doubt transient, unsatisfactory and non-self. Ultimately, full realisation of this leads the mind to turn

---

[1] Pure abodes: a group of 5 heavens belonging to the fine material world (*rūpa-loka*).

away from the relative world, and to seek perfection in the signless, the beyond, *nibbāna*.

☆ ☆ ☆

So much for the systematic approach. Using every technique available, the meditator has broken through the blindness of ignorance and arrived at his destination. However, the system culminating in *vipassanā* does not lead to enlightenment, but to a mind-created imitation of it. The path leads to a mind-created resultant state called a fruition. It is signless, but it is man-made, and the opposite of the state with signs, which is our usual condition.

The Buddha taught an extraordinarily effective system, a system that works just as well today as it has done – every day – over the past two and a half thousand years. He also taught a non-system. He taught many ways finally to overcome reliance upon systems of any kind – including the system, Dhamma, which he himself so enthusiastically propounded. The Buddha instructed his students first to reach the signless, and then to examine that achievement and to transcend even that.

In one discourse, the Buddha said (speaking of a meditator who had reached the fruition of *vipassanā*),

'His mind is satisfied with, pleased with, set on and freed in the concentration of mind that is signless. He comprehends, "There is only this degree of disturbance – that is to say, the six sensory fields that, conditioned by life, are grounded on this body itself." Further, he comprehends, "This concentration of mind that is signless is effected [in other words, man-made] and thought out. But whatever is thought out is impermanent, and liable to stopping."

'When he knows this, sees this, his mind is freed from the canker of sense-pleasures; his mind is freed from the canker of becoming; his mind is freed from the canker of ignorance. In freedom is the knowledge that he is freed, and he comprehends, "Destroyed is birth, brought to a close is the Brahma-faring, done is what was to be done, there is no more of being such or so."'

[*Middle Length Sayings* Sutta No 121 §109]

The Teaching of the Buddha provides a complete and fully

documented path to the highest of man's aspirations. It provides systematic and penetrative analysis of the human condition, and a way to go beyond even that – to complete freedom. It is the royal road to the cessation of suffering.

15

THE UNFOLDING OF WISDOM

The development of intellectual right view is an essential step on the way to freedom, but not enough on its own. Nothing can be gained without insight, which transcends intellect altogether. Right view, or seeing, as direct observation of reality, is indispensable; it **has** to be developed if freedom is to be won. Intellectual right view is a supporting condition; insight is a necessary condition.

Insight can be persuaded to arise only through actual, experiential observation of the workings of mind and body, and this observation must be combined with clear perception of the three marks of all conditioned existence. This is true meditation. Without experiencing for yourself the reality of transience, unsatisfactoriness and non-self (*anicca, dukkha* and *anattā*), nothing happens, no freedom is won, you remain bound to the wheel of *samsāra* with no way off.

Meditation is no easy task, neither when one chooses first to develop deeply concentrated states nor when one opts instead for the seemingly faster method of 'dry' insight, *vipassanā* on its own. There is much preparation in either case: adapting one's behaviour, if necessary, to conform to the five precepts; learning about the constitution of the human being in terms of mind and body; learning about conditioning; learning about hindrances and how to put them aside.

While individual meditators vary greatly in the ease with which they familiarise themselves with the training, there is nevertheless a common path along which all of them walk. Through personal restraint via the five precepts, each meditator comes to an increasing familiarity with ease of mind gained through self-discipline. Restraining the senses and developing the capacity to suppress the hindrances, he begins to experience relative freedom of mind that makes the practice of insight meditation a real possibility. It is only at this point that he can start to plumb the hidden recesses of mind. Only after the preparatory work can he effectively seek the elusive truth of things as they are.

I would like to examine a typical meditator's progress from the point when he is able, more or less at will, to suppress the hindrances. Once the hindrances can be suppressed the meditation takes on quite a different aspect. Gone are the sometimes despairing struggles to pursue elusive clarity. Now the practice is bright and sharp, with experience thrown into sharp relief in the most detailed manner. It feels as if one has burst the shackles restricting the mind and all is at last possible.

The step leading to this happy state of affairs is called 'knowledge of overcoming doubt'. As its name suggests, this stage can be very trying, for it may be beset by doubts about what you are attempting and is often accompanied by physical aches and pains. Often in meditation practice there is a period of difficulty that did the student but know it, heralds a breakthrough into calmer and clearer waters.

The essence of overcoming doubt is coming to see clearly, through experience, for the first time, that consciousness arises dependent solely upon an object and that there is no 'self' necessary to the process. The meditator is aware of, say, a visual object, then seeing consciousness, then mind consciousness following on immediately. He sees, clearly and unmistakeably, that there is in that complex of conditioned states no 'self'; there is simply consciousness arising in dependence on an object. That is all there is. That is all there has ever been.

With the right level of concentration and attention it is possible to experience this for yourself, to know for a fact that this is the way it is. This leads to the understanding that this whole complex life, from birth to death, is nothing but consciousness arising dependent on an object. The whole history of the world that we believe to exist, the whole universe itself – when examined through the searchlight of pure mind – is seen and understood to be nothing but consciousness arising dependent on an object. There is in all this experience – past, present and future – no self, no me, no I, no other. There is simply consciousness arising dependent on an object.

'Knowledge of overcoming doubt' by understanding conditionality is a significant point to reach in the meditation.

The following stage is even more important. Known as 'knowledge of arising and passing away', it is here that the path to enlightenment starts in earnest. Some call this stage on the path 'lesser stream-winner', saying that anyone getting to this point is certain to become enlightened within, perhaps, a hundred or so lifetimes. From here it is possible to go on to establish true insight into the three marks of all conditioned existence as well as complete knowledge of the four noble truths.

If you have strongly developed powers of concentration, it would be at this point that you might divert into developing the jhanas, the fixed meditations, and possibly the psychic powers. You might, for instance, develop a mental body, the exact duplicate of the physical, but able to walk through walls, to swim in the earth, to fly through the air and to visit far-off places.

You might develop the divine eye and thus be able to see things happening at a distance; or the divine ear, allowing you to hear things normally beyond the scope of the physical ear. It is at this point, too, that someone might choose to develop the capacity to investigate his or her past lives, or to watch the way in which other beings die and are reborn according to their deeds. Another of the psychic powers is to know the minds of others, to know what they are thinking or what their moods are. All these things are possible, given sufficient development.

The psychic powers so far mentioned are not in any way necessary for enlightenment, although they can be of great assistance in finding out the 'why?' and the 'how?' of things. There is one power, however, that leads to supramundane knowledge, to wisdom, to the destruction of the passions of craving and hatred. The development of this psychic power can be accomplished only by seeing the three marks – transience, unsatisfactoriness and non-self – in everything, in the most exquisite detail, with the fullest penetration of the mind it is possible to acquire.

When the marks are truly seen and experienced in this way, it becomes obvious that there really never was any thing to crave or hate; that all craving and hatred is based on a misconception, on a wrong idea, on a wrong belief. With this illumination gained through direct experience, confusion dies away, it vanishes. Craving can never arise again, for the truth of things is seen.

With full awareness of the three marks of all conditioned phenomena, knowledge of the four noble truths comes to fruition. If one discounts the years of preparation for this moment, it happens in an instant. *nibbāna* is glimpsed for the first time. In retrospect and in contrast it becomes obvious that there is suffering in the world; indeed, how could it be otherwise? It also becomes obvious that the cause of this suffering is craving. Where there is craving, there has to be suffering – for craving, any craving, is craving for the impossible: for things that do not exist, that cannot exist, that never have existed. It is ignorance of this fact that keeps us in thrall to suffering and misery, no matter how conventionally happy our lives might appear.

The moment when *nibbāna* is seen for the first time is known as a fruition (*phala*). It is the result of all the meditative work that has been done so far. A fruition is an important milestone on the journey to enlightenment, for it marks the destruction of some of the fetters that bind us to *samsāra*. There are four fruitions, one at the end of each of four paths. A meditator achieving the fruitions is called, in order, a stream-winner, a once-returner, a non-returner and an *arahant*.

If he does no more meditative work, the stream-winner has at most only seven more lifetimes before full enlightenment. The once-returner comes back, as the name suggests, only one more time to this scheme of things. The non-returner is reborn in the 'pure abodes', there to realise enlightenment, and the *arahant* has completed the task and is to be reborn no more.

Each path consists of the very same stages of development, but at successively more subtle levels. Each addresses different obstacles or fetters, finally to eradicate them. For the record, I should list the fetters for you. They are:

Eradicated by the first path and fruition
    1. Belief in a self
    2. Sceptical doubt
    3. Clinging to rule and ritual

Eradicated by the second path and fruition
    4. Gross sensual craving
    5. Gross ill-will

Eradicated by the third path and fruition
    4. Subtle sensual craving
    5. Subtle ill-will

Eradicated by the fourth path and fruition
    6. Craving for fine-material existence
    7. Craving for non-material existence
    8. Conceit
    9. Restlessness
  10. Ignorance

The first five fetters are called 'those that bind to the lower world (*kāma-loka*)'; one who has overcome all five is a non-returner.

Each fruition is a mind-produced state: it is a resultant state that mimics *nibbāna*, and not the final goal of the path. This applies even to the fourth and final fruition, which many believe to mark complete enlightenment. These resultant states are, like 'real' *nibbāna*, signless, but they are unquestionably produced by the preceding efforts of the meditator. There is still a leap of understanding to be made before enlightenment is truly won.

I suppose it is reasonable to ask how fruitions could possibly eradicate fetters if they are imitations of the real thing. The way it works is this. As the meditative journey progresses, it becomes impossible to fool yourself that, for instance, reciting a mantra or performing endless prostrations – or meditating sixteen hours a day, for that matter – will **of themselves** lead to the freedom from suffering that is *nibbāna*. Thus the fetter of adherence to rule and ritual is overcome.

In a similar vein, observation of the conditioned and transient nature of every experienceable aspect, 'component' or process of mind and body leads to the inescapable conclusion that belief in a permanent self is unwarranted. Thus the first fetter is broken.

Glimpsing *nibbāna*, even in its 'counterfeit' form, is quite sufficient to prove that it does exist and that it is truly the cessation of suffering. With such understanding, the second fetter, that of sceptical doubt, is similarly eliminated.

I know that it runs contrary to accepted wisdom but the *arahant* – defined as someone who has experienced the fourth fruition – is **not** thereby fully enlightened. Usually, he or she still has one more concept to deal with: the concept of being enlightened. Dealing with this last most recalcitrant of concepts precipitates true and complete enlightenment. **Then** can the enlightened individual truly claim to have burst the bonds, broken the fetters, overcome the floods and put away the cankers. Then can he or she claim truly to have arrived at the other shore. It is then that the whole picture becomes clear. Enlightenment is known and understood and in that enlightenment there is the certain knowledge that the task is complete. Before this the meditator was always concerned in some way whether he had got it right.

Enlightenment is not a calm, always 'blissed-out' state – but one where there is no suffering of any kind, no matter what bodily or mental upset there may be. There is absolutely no craving, or hatred, concerning discomforts – and thus no suffering at all.

Enlightenment is to come to understand that there never was, never has been, never is and never will be any division, separation or dichotomy. Simply, there is only this – which is non-dual. This is all there is. And yet, if you think about it, and talk about it, you always fall into error; you always make mistakes.

Enlightenment is to come to see that things never have been any different. That whatever you do, or do not do, you are inextricably part of all there is. More accurately, no matter what you choose to think, do or say, there never has been any division or separation.

Enlightenment is to bring the understanding of perfection even into the most mundane of activities. It is not to lose sight of perfection, even in the midst of anguish, torture, and disaster – physical or emotional. Understanding the perfection of imperfection is the wisdom, the strength and the wonder of those who have gone beyond – those who are truly most worthy.

It becomes blindingly obvious that the beyond, the escape from suffering, is nothing other than the destruction of craving itself. The destruction of craving is the escape from suffering.

The fourth truth, that there is a way leading to the cessation of suffering, comes brilliantly to life with the destruction of craving. Having reached the beyond, it is plain to see that there is in fact a way to it, and that you have just travelled along it. You have discovered that the whole course of training is, as it claims, the way to enlightenment. All your questions as to the 'why?' of suffering and happiness are resolved.

Other things, though, remain forever a mystery; and those are perhaps the subject of another talk. The Buddha enumerated ten speculations not answered by the Teaching:

> 'Is the world eternal ... not eternal?; is the world an ending thing ... not an ending thing?; is the life principle the same as the body ... not the same as the body?; does the Tathagata [the Buddha] exist after dying ... not exist after dying ... both exist and not exist ... neither exist nor not exist after dying?'
>
> [*Middle Length Sayings* Sutta No 63]

He also outlined four areas of which one can never properly grasp the extent, the 'four unthinkables': the sphere of Buddhas; the sphere of one practising the jhanas; the results of *kamma*; the origins and future of the world.

The unfolding of wisdom is a matter apart from these imponderables. In short, it is that all suffering, all distress, all disaffection, all dissatisfaction is completely eradicated and there is nothing more to do. The journey is ended and life can live but no one needs to be troubled by it. You have come to understand why man searches for the 'why?' of things, and why he goes on a spiritual search in the first place. You have come to the place sages of every age call home, and it is as eternally fresh now as it has ever been.

16

CONCEPTS OF ENLIGHTENMENT

While enlightenment is without question possible today, it nevertheless remains an enigma. It cannot be described with any accuracy and yet millions of words have been generated trying to convey just how worthwhile a goal it is. Man has given it many different names, but always the same difficulties attend a description. Often, description of the thing-in-itself is abandoned in favour of a portrayal of those who have come to know for themselves this reality behind appearances. Even here difficulties abound, for what is predicated of the enlightened person is always viewed from a limited point of view and, as such, is hardly accurate. However, there definitely are certain things that can be said, even if many of them are in the negative.

The discourse that begins *Middle Length Sayings*, The Synopsis of Fundamentals, is of particular value when we attempt to distinguish the differences between 'ordinary' (*puthujjana*) people and those who are enlightened – not to mention those in between, people under training. It states that the ordinary person 'rejoices in *nibbana*, thinks of self in regard to *nibbāna*, and thinks, "*Nibbāna* is mine,"' – whereas the enlightened person just does not think in terms of self at all.

The uninstructed average worldling, the discourse tells us, recognises *nibbāna*, or the element of heat – or anything else at all, and thinks, 'This is me, this is mine, this is the self of me.' The person in training, in contrast, deliberately applies his mind to the same objects, thinking, 'This is not me, this is not mine, this is not the self of me.' The person who is fully trained, the enlightened person, does not think, 'This is me, this is mine, this is the self of me.' Nor does he think, 'This is not me, this is not mine, this is not the self of me.' He has gone quite beyond all concern with self, either positive or negative.

All individuals experience the ultimate elements of existence.

Everyone experiences hardness and softness, heat and cold. Everyone experiences *nibbāna*. It is the interpretation of these experiences that varies dramatically across the spectrum of people, from unenlightened to enlightened. The 'uninstructed average worldling' always thinks of experience in terms of me and mine, and in terms of permanence and satisfactoriness. In complete contrast, the enlightened person does not; he never thinks in terms of me or mine. The person in the middle, the one in training, applies the counteractive perceptions of transience, unsatisfactoriness and non-self to all experience. Meditation on transience is the key to the transition from uninstructed average worldling to enlightened being.

The 'uninstructed average worldling' is unaware of the rigorous nature of experiential analysis that dispels illusions. If he has thought about such things at all, he often holds peculiar ideas about enlightenment and about enlightened beings. I want to look at some of these wrong ideas to see if we can identify the errors in thinking that give rise to them.

☆ ☆ ☆

Some believe that enlightenment is a matter of goodness – of skilful or ethically efficient action only, as opposed to understanding.

Such people are enthusiastic about the morality of Buddhism and suggest, for instance, that you have to be vegetarian to become enlightened, as though it were an absolute requirement. Such a stance completely misses the point of the Buddha's Teaching, which is expressly not to provide a set of absolute rules by which to live, but to come to the total cessation of suffering. Rule and ritual, while helpful in their own place, are limited to the relative world and never got anyone to the beyond. Attachment to them forms a fetter that binds us to the unenlightened state.

If you want the understanding that brings total cessation of all suffering, then Buddha Dhamma, the Teaching of the Buddha, gives you a way to get it: insight meditation. The path rests, of necessity, on developed ethical behaviour – on behaviour that is truly efficient, in the sense of producing calm and happiness. This foundation produces sufficient tranquillity of mind to start your journey, but that journey itself has very little to do with rule and ritual. It is a common misconception, now as then, that *nibbāna* is somehow the acme of moral or ethical observance.

Another common idea is that enlightened beings know everything, they are omniscient.

Can you imagine how it would be possible suddenly to acquire with no previous study a perfect and in-depth knowledge of nuclear physics, microtonic scales or quadratic equations? It cannot be done, whoever you are. It takes years of diligent application to become expert in even one field of knowledge, let alone several. The amount of information in the world is infinite; no one could ever in a million, million years know all there is to know. That sort of information, that sort of so-called knowledge, has nothing to do with enlightenment at all. The enlightened person, like anyone else, may be quite ignorant in conventional terms. Education, in the modern Western sense, has literally nothing to do with enlightenment and the search for true wisdom.

Another belief is that enlightened people relate perfectly with others.

Most understand people very well, but some cannot stand relating to them, preferring solitude instead. Others may understand them well and love company, preferring to relate to others wherever possible. It all depends upon the individual's past conditioning in this area.

The development of any mundane skill depends upon much hard work in the appropriate field. Whether you aim to be a great mathematician, a great politician or even a master criminal, all such skills take a great amount of dedication and work in a series of lives, not to mention this one. Psychic power follows the same rules. If you spend lifetimes developing the psychic powers then it is hardly surprising if, in your final lifetime, you acquire psychic abilities even if you do not specifically seek them. If you have never had any particular interest in such powers, however, then you will not 'suddenly' develop them.

In reality you never suddenly develop anything. Any apparently sudden development rests on past endeavours. It takes a long, long time to set in new abilities, especially of any complexity or subtlety. Even supported by past-life experience, it takes protracted effort, much of it, to establish new levels of proficiency. The ability to relate well to people is just such a skill and takes a great amount of work to perfect.

Many believe that enlightened beings have perfect health, that

they never fall ill or feel indisposed. Allied with this is the view
that they never need to sleep. Some go so far as to suggest that
they do not need even to eat, being able somehow to transmute
from the atmosphere the nutrients needed to sustain physical
life. Extending the idea of perfect health, some believe the
enlightened to possess the secret of physical immortality.

The concept that if you are spiritually advanced, you must
always be perfectly healthy, even physically immortal, is very
difficult to square with the death of enlightened individuals such
as the Buddha and his arahants. Nevertheless, it is a very
common view and so attractive that many prefer it to reality. For
these adherents, someone's death is taken as proof that he or she
could not have been enlightened in the first place.

There is a view, prevalent perhaps more in Oriental countries
but still current here in the West, that enlightened beings are
always men. I can assure you, from personal experience and a
great deal of research as well, that historically and currently that
is definitely not so.

Some hold that everybody would know that someone is
enlightened. They believe the enlightened individual must be so
distinctive, so charismatic, so compassionate, so kind, so wise, so
long-lived, so positive, that he or she must stand out from the
crowd and be visible to everyone.

While some enlightened beings may be charismatic, like the
Buddha, such personal magnetism has nothing to do with
enlightenment. In the Pali Canon (always worth reading, and re-
reading), the enlightened being is described as 'trackless, like a
bird in the sky'. Why? Because he or she is such an indivisible
part of reality, so perfectly blended with all there is, as to leave
no trace at all. There is nothing by which you can mark the track
of such an individual, for he or she is not a physical, mental,
psychic or ethical giant. Put another way, enlightenment cannot
be measured; it is not accessible to rulers and gauges, nor
signified by badges and banners.

Another common view is that an enlightened person does not
indulge in sex. A variant of this view is that the enlightened are
incapable of any sexual activity at all, because they have no
craving left.

This view stems from a complete misunderstanding of the
way the body functions and of the difference between craving
(*tanhā*) and desire-to-do (*chanda*). Craving is a kammically active

lust – for anything, including sex; it is associated with ignorance of the three marks and of the four noble truths and has as its resultant suffering. Desire-to-do, on the other hand, is ethically neutral, may be associated with any activity and has nothing to do with craving or hatred.

It is indeed true that an enlightened, ordained recluse would be incapable of sexual activity – but not because of physical inability. An enlightened monk or nun would not break the rules by which the order lives. The rules enjoin complete celibacy; the enlightened comply. Enlightened people not under such constraints, lay people perhaps, or those in communities that do not have such restrictive rules, do what they wish in this matter.

Moving away from matters of the body into the realm of the mind, many believe that enlightened beings invariably possess psychic powers.

Sometimes they do, but not necessarily. Sometimes people acquire psychic powers with enlightenment, but in relatively few cases is that so. Some accept that an enlightened individual is not fully psychic, but believe he gained a certain degree of mind-reading with enlightenment. This, too, is not necessarily so. A reputation for mental powers may be based on unrecognised observational skills. Some individuals are completely deaf and blind on the psychic level but can infer with great accuracy what is going in another's mind. They make their deductions by virtue of experience; reading body language, eye signals, words, sentence construction, that kind of thing. Such inference may be completely accurate and yet have nothing in it of mind-reading at all.

Many hold the view that enlightened individuals are always calm; that they never get angry, they never show irritation or any such 'negative' states.

In the Pali Canon you will find there are numerous occasions where the Buddha took to task an errant monk and said to him, 'You foolish man! How could you do such a thing?' He gave every outward demonstration of anger, irritation, annoyance. To the recipient, the Buddha's response may have been indistinguishable from anger. For someone who has eradicated craving and hatred, however, anger-based-on-self-view is not possible. The state of 'enlightened anger' has no thought of self or non-self. It is utterly different from its unenlightened equivalent, which is always bound up with ignorance and belief in the existence of a self.

Some say that to be enlightened you have to be born that way. Thus ordinary mortals have no chance.

This may stem from the Hindu concept of the *avatar*, an incarnation or emanation of God, and seems a perfect excuse for avoiding the spiritual search. Yet to be born enlightened would be possible, if at all, only if the individual had done the vast amount of unavoidable preparatory work in his or her previous lifetimes.

This view seems to me similar to the idea that there is no enlightened being in existence today. In spite of all the evidence to the contrary, there are many who maintain that enlightenment is impossible in modern times. I have heard with my own ears a prominent Buddhist teacher say publicly that there may, just may, be stream-winners living in distant caves in the Himalayas. Indicating that this was a wonderful dream and only remotely possible, he clearly thought that the meditative path was very unlikely to succeed today, even though he was a monk of a lifetime's standing.

Such a view devalues the entire meditative path: why bother to work at it if you think there is no chance of success? What is the attraction in a life of extremely challenging work, being brought face to face with your own ignorance at every step, if you are going to get nothing out of it except pain and suffering? Based on this view only masochists would seek ordination – or perhaps those believing the recluse's life is a soft option, or a way to gain respect in the community.

There are many and various concepts of enlightenment and the enlightened individual. Without exception they are inaccurate – simply because they are concepts. It is very helpful, however, to try to refine one's view of enlightenment, to come as close as possible to the truth. This can help to shed light on the more obvious inconsistencies and bring one closer to real understanding. In a sense the whole of the path is to try to define just what is meant by the cessation of suffering, the beyond, *nibbāna*. This **is** the quest and the answer is realised by a combination of intellectual enquiry and rigorous experiential analysis of one's world. There is nothing more worthwhile, nothing more rewarding, for this is man's purpose and his destiny.

17

DEFINING THE INDEFINABLE

In *Middle Length Sayings* there is a discourse, No 28, The Simile of the Elephant's Footprint, which contains the sentence, 'Whatever is material shape in what has thus come to be, it is included in the group of grasping after material shape.' This states that whenever material shape arises, of whatever kind, past, present or future, it is included within the *khandha* of – the group of grasping after – materiality. This clearly implies that there is **grasping** in the normal sensory process, in this case of sight.

Some find this confusing, believing, wrongly, that material shape is always there but the grasping is there only occasionally. If you differentiate a material shape, you do a violence to the universe – which does not include material shape. Material shape is something arbitrarily separated from an indivisible reality. Grasping at it, you delineate it and create it in that very moment. Dividing the indivisible by grasping, you create something that is truly unsatisfactory; you create suffering, for the creation of the material shape is attended by a belief that such a thing exists as a reality.

Some argue that the enlightened person experiences material shape when there is contact between eye and visible object (material shape). In reality, however, there is no contact. Contact is only possible between a self (or an 'I'), a differentiated organ and a differentiated object, treated as real things. Such contact is possible only if you believe in duality, in the existence of separate things. This is the view of *attā*, of the existence of self: the belief that things exist; that I exist, that eye exists, that material shapes exist as unchanging entities. It is the old, old belief in the duality of self and other, of subject and object.

When that belief is utterly rooted out; when there is no more the idea of self and other – and that includes eye and material shape; when all of that is entirely gone, that is enlightenment.

How then can you talk about material shape and eye? You cannot, because you know that those things are not real, they do not exist. This is the point where language fails, and unless we are all prepared to talk in less than precise terms, nothing more can be said.

The Buddha spoke of the 'signless', saying that the uncreated signless – as distinct from that brought about by mental endeavour – was the goal (*Middle Length Sayings* Sutta No 121). The signless is that 'state' where no signs exist; it is specifically the absence of the three marks or signs of impermanence, unsatisfactoriness and non-self. Again we have the clear implication that nothing may be predicated of the beyond without falling into an error of description, for all description assumes at least some permanence, if nothing else.

The problem with such strict definition is that it leaves the enquiring mind dissatisfied, for there is nothing left at which to grasp. This leads some to suppose that enlightenment must be annihilation – which it most definitely is not; or that it does not exist – which, assuredly, it does.

People needed to be reassured that the enlightened state was a positive and worthwhile goal. Although they could see people said to be enlightened walking, talking and living normally among them, purely negative descriptions worried them. To say that someone had utterly eradicated craving, hatred and confusion did not demonstrate what they experienced **now**.

Other descriptions of the enlightened state aggravated this concern. For instance, Sariputta, one of the Buddha's two chief disciples, commented that the beauty of enlightenment is that there are no sensations, sounds, smells and the like.

This confused most people. After all, enlightened people manifestly were not unconscious, at least in conventional terms – even if one description of *nibbāna* is the cessation of consciousness – so there had to be some kind of mental process occurring. Didn't there?

Although the Buddha always taught that *nibbāna* was a *dhamma*, a 'thing' that could be experienced, it was understood that this was for the purposes of instruction, and to distinguish it from *samsāra*, the world of suffering. After all, he needed to talk about something that is 'unnameable' and beyond all concepts and so needed an appropriate term.

He took this idea further by dividing *nibbāna* into two

varieties: *nibbāna* with the groups (*khandha*) remaining and *nibbāna* without the groups remaining. The latter defines the 'state' of the enlightened person after death, when the groups, mind and body, are no longer in existence. The former describes the enlightened individual – enlightened, certainly, but still, relatively speaking, subject to the vagaries of sensory existence, although without craving, hatred or ignorance.

Expanding this idea, the groups (*khandha*) themselves needed to be classified in two different ways: groups subject to grasping (*upādāna*) and groups not so afflicted. This logical device makes it possible to talk about the experience of the enlightened person in terms that are comprehensible by those still bound to the wheel of rebirth. In my experience it also introduces a difficulty for those under training, for the following reasons. Firstly, it suggests that enlightenment is 'only' a matter of learning to live within an imperfect world by adopting a stoic and uncomplaining frame of mind. Secondly, it enhances the belief that the highest goal is gained by control – of the hindrances and of perception – rather than by the spontaneous transcendence of all views and structures.

Accepting the idea of two kinds of *nibbāna*, you can say that the enlightened being does see 'material shape', but there is for him absolutely no belief in its permanence or its reality. In the words of the Japanese saying, after enlightenment, 'Once again men are men, mountains are mountains and trees are trees – but no one is confused by the terms.' Before the realisation of the beyond, however, everyone is to a certain extent confused by the terms and believes material shape, mountains and trees to be real things. It is at that level that 'whatever is material shape is included in the group of grasping after material shape', for one is grasping at it as a reality, as something separate from other things.

For the unenlightened person there is always an element of grasping: it is just a matter of degree. Even if there are moments when, for the unenlightened person, there is no grasping, then **subsequent** moments look back on them with grasping.

In The Synopsis of Fundamentals in *Middle Length Sayings* (Sutta No 1), the Buddha says that there is essentially no difference between the ordinary person and the enlightened person, except in one critically important area: the enlightened person is the one who **knows** that there is no difference. There is a long list: the *puthujjana*, the worldling, is aware of extension, cohesion, temperature, contact, feeling, and so on, up to and including *nibbāna*; and thinks, 'This is me, this is mine, this is the self of me.' The enlightened person is aware of extension, cohesion, temperature, contact, feeling and so on, up to and including *nibbāna*; but he does not think, never even has the tendency to think, 'This is me, this is mine, this is the self of me.' This is the essential difference.

It is very subtle, and it begins to show as clearly as nothing else can that the Dhamma, *paticca-samuppāda*, Condition Dependent Origination, is dealing with the ignorant universe; it is dealing with the universe as seen from an unenlightened standpoint.

The Dhamma has been called the supreme dialectic because ultimately it destroys even itself. As a description of the world, it is so refined and so perfect that if you use it as a basis for practice, you get to the point where it transcends itself; you leave it behind, like the raft that the Buddha called it. You leave behind even the most pristine element of the ignorant world and leap into something that cannot be described. *Nibbāna*, the Buddha said, is the place where the four elements earth, air, fire and water (extension, motion, temperature and cohesion) find no footing at all; they cannot exist there.

Saying what enlightenment is not and where views about it are mistaken is one thing. Illustrating the positive aspects of enlightenment in a way that does not confuse the entire issue is quite another.

There are several different approaches to the dilemma of describing the non-dual in terms of the dual. One is to explain just how conventional or even ultimate descriptions of the universe do not really apply when talking about enlightenment. It is, after all, entirely beyond the scheme of things with which we believe ourselves to be so familiar. The familiar world of things and experiences, all grasped at, is transcended by insight. Insight proves conclusively that all previous ways of perceiving the world were in error. What is left then? Can it be properly described – or do words fail? We might take another tack and say that *samsāra* and *nibbāna* are the same (but, clearly, different – or we would not have to say so); or that the beyond is 'empty' of all phenomena (but not nothing), and other paradoxical statements.

To assist in the quest for understanding, the Buddha spoke often of *nibbāna*, the goal of the meditative training. He called it by various names: the deathless, the highest bliss, the cessation of suffering, the beyond, the 'unborn, uncreated and unbecome'. *Nibbāna*, he said, is not affected by the number of people who become enlightened, nor is the enlightenment of a student different from that of a master, including the Buddha himself.

He employed different methods when trying to convey the truly alien nature of the enlightened state – alien, that is, from the point of view of the 'uninstructed average worldling ', the *puthujjana*.

The Buddha said, 'He who sees Dhamma, sees me; he who sees me, sees Dhamma.' This implies that the enlightened person embodies the law of life and cannot be separated from it in any way. His statement also indicates that whoever sees the law of life, sees enlightenment (*buddha*); he or she becomes enlightened.

A true understanding of Dhamma brings the realisation that it is impossible to break that law even in the smallest way. It becomes obvious that all suffering, dissatisfaction, anguish, sorrow and despair – whether past, present or future – arise from the ignorant attempt to break the unbreakable, to perform the impossible, to think the unthinkable. Thus it is true to say that the Buddha, the man, embodies the law of life, is the law of life, is Dhamma; and if you understand the Buddha, you understand the law of life, you understand his Teaching. If you understand his Teaching, you understand the Buddha, you understand enlightenment. It gets to the point where the two are in a sense not separate.

Enlightenment is perfection and, as such, contains all there is, including suffering and all views of self. Everyone is in fact 'enlightened' – but most are unaware that they are perfect as they are. However, none of this helps very much when it comes to a determined effort to unravel the secrets of the universe. It is cold comfort to be told that *samsāra* and *nibbāna* are the same if there is no way to see that for yourself.

Study of the teachings is a necessary and unavoidable step if we are really to make progress on the way to freedom. Gaining an intellectual understanding of the precise analysis of human experience into perceptible patterns is of immense benefit in the meditation. Such understanding helps greatly to overcome the internal hindrances; it also helps us to discriminate experience at the ultimate level. Clear discrimination of ultimate experience allows us to see how mind works and to develop restraint – especially of unhelpful personal reactions that cloud our ability to see the true nature of reality.

Continued observation leads to the recognition that mental restraint can never be sufficient, no matter how skilful. It becomes clear by default that understanding is the key to the beyond. Increasing insight culminates in the wisdom that sees the unsatisfactory nature of the relative, conditioned world. Turning aside, the mind leaps for the unknown, bursting free of the prison of conditioning it has chosen to endure for lifetime after lifetime. *Nibbāna* is seen and the fetters of ignorance are broken forever.

18

ESCAPE FROM SAMSARA

The Buddha often spoke to his followers of the cycle of birth and death called *samsāra*, perpetual wandering. He said we are born now here, now there, in different lives and planes of existence, never able to find any stable resting place; always moving on from death to birth, endlessly. In a graphic description, he said that were they not to decay, the bones from all the bodies one of us has had throughout the ages would make a mountain higher than Everest. He spoke also about birth and death in the moment, saying that every time the sense-of-self comes into existence that too is a birth followed by inevitable death.

Continual change gives us a chance, should we want it, to reach out for different, more exalted states of being. As no state is permanent there is always the chance to improve. And yet improvement is, really, just more of the same. Anything we can achieve is ephemeral. Everything is transient. Everything is unsatisfactory.

The heart of the Buddha's message is that there is an escape from this unsatisfactoriness. All suffering can utterly cease. There is beyond *samsāra* something that is perfection itself. This is the deathless, *nibbāna*, the goal of the Buddha's Teaching. This is enlightenment, the cessation of suffering.

There is the world we appear to live in, with all its different levels of existence, and beyond it there is the 'unborn, uncreated, unbecome'. We seem forever to be separated from this beyond, this enlightenment, but the separation is apparent rather than real.

Consider a television set. To look at, it consists essentially of a glass screen and a few controls. But switch it on and that unremarkable screen suddenly fills with moving images. Now the only things visible are the pictures. Even if you look for the screen itself it is hard to make out; the images are normally so dominant. It is as if there were two kinds of reality running in parallel. There is the screen, which is always present, yet unnoticed, and there are the pictures, highly visible and attractive, yet which have no substance and no duration.

The conventional world of *samsāra*, the world of birth and death, just like the pictures on the screen, is transient in every detail. If you believe the pictures to be reality itself, you will inevitably be disappointed and unfulfilled. If you realise they are a kind of fantasy, valid in their own terms but only tenuously related to the real world, then you will not be so deluded by appearances and will suffer far less.

Birth in the moment-to-moment sense is like the coming into existence of a recognisable picture on the television screen. At this point we are unaware of the screen itself to the extent that you could say that for us it does not exist; our attention is so caught by the moving images that the screen is obscured and ignored.

None of the images we take to be important is 'real' in the sense of having an actual or lasting existence. There is nothing we can do to control them, and whether they are portraying something we enjoy or something we hate, nothing we can do makes any difference to what is taking place in the moment. If we get so caught up in the plot that it becomes as though real life for us, it is exactly like the life we lead in *samsāra*: it seems as if it is the only thing that exists. At that time we are totally ignorant of the reality of the screen.

What is true of the television is also true of life itself. Birth is the coming into existence of a recognisable picture. It is the moment at which we 'fix' the flux of life and say, 'This is a tree,' or 'This is a mountain,' or 'This is my self.' Having created a mountain or a tree in the moment, we then act as though it had some kind of permanent reality.

When the real event, due to the processes of natural change, becomes too different from the picture we created in the first place, we then say that the thing has 'changed'. We forget that there really was no 'thing' in the first place; we just **said** there was. If the thing changes so much that it becomes totally unrecognisable, then we say it 'dies' or ceases. But what dies? What we mean is that the image we created is now so far out of date that it does not bear any relation at all to reality.

Ignorance, or blindness, is the waywardness of human

thought that insists that we are right, that there really was 'something' to die. It is to forget completely that we invented the 'thing' in the first place. There was nothing static in reality; we just grasped at – and falsely isolated – an aspect of dynamic experience. No thing actually existed then. No thing exists now. It never existed at all – except in the realms of fantasy, like the pictures on the TV screen.

It is true that pictures always did exist and always will. That is not the problem. The problem lies in believing that the pictures are of real and unchanging things. When there is a belief in the reality of the pictures there grows up all the suffering in the world. Without that belief there is no problem at all.

'Birth' can only be associated with an ignorance of the true state of affairs. In reality there is no-thing to be born. It is as though we take a photograph of an apple falling from a tree or a wave breaking on a beach and then claim that it always exists in just that state and no other.

Death also is nothing, for there is nothing to die. There are only 'pictures on a screen'. No part of the picture is a permanent reality. It is all constantly in flux, the patterns ever-changing. The screen stays the same and is completely unaffected by the pictures. The pictures come and go. Placing all our devotion on the pictures, we completely miss the existence of the screen. We live in a world of transience and suffering born of ignorance and attachment to phantoms. This is *samsāra*. This is the world of birth and death. This is what has to be transcended if we are to come to the end of suffering.

We stay attached to our wrong view of the world only because we perceive things as lasting. Seeing that things around us appear to last for varying lengths of time, we come to assume that some of them – the 'self' for instance – are so lasting that they never die. We falsely perceive things of the world to be permanent, satisfactory and isolated from one another. From this false view arises craving and all possible suffering.

We stay attached to our beliefs just as long as we do not see the truth of 'things as they are'. *Vipassanā* meditation allows us to penetrate below the surface of the things we think we know. This meditation produces in-sight knowledge that begins to break down preconceived notions.

Insight meditation removes false view by allowing the individual to see clearly. Firstly you learn to perceive the different aspects of mind and body; you learn discrimination to see properly just what is taking place. Secondly, you examine all those different processes and phenomena with the trained eye of attention.

You have to be really concerned to find out the truth. You have to remark strongly to yourself when you see that something passes away, so that you impress the fact of impermanence clearly on the mind. Time, perseverance and careful systematic attention will show that everything you attend to is transient. Nothing lasts.

When the insight that nothing lasts becomes strongly enough established, the mind begins to turn away from all the things it has previously delighted in. It becomes disenchanted by the fantasy and the attachment formerly so important. Eventually it forsakes altogether the limited and mundane world and takes for its object the unconditioned element itself. It leaps into *nibbāna*, leaving far, far behind the entire mundane universe with its heavens and hells. It goes beyond *samsāra* and comes to understand the truth of things as they are. This is enlightenment. This is the cessation of suffering. This is to come to the end of birth and death.

☆ ☆ ☆

The journey is over. The top of the mountain is reached. The burden is finally put down. There is no more to do. You see now that there was never any need to travel to find what you sought; it is here always. In fact it is not possible ever to get away from it. You could say that you are it, but there never was a 'you' in the first place. There was never an 'it', either. Anything you say is not true – it is just more pictures on the screen. This is the eternal silence: it is not that there is no sound, but that there is nothing to say. Everything is perfect as it is.

If you do try to put into words this most transcendental of experiences you run into overwhelming difficulties. You know now that words like 'self' and 'other', 'mountain' and 'tree', do not mean anything. You know they can never mean anything. And yet what is there is not nothing. This is freedom. This is to see things as they are. This is to have come to the end of the task.

INDEX

BUDDHISM IN A FOREIGN LAND

Robert Mann

As Buddhism is taking root in the West, evolving new forms to suit new conditions, much of its traditional oriental context is being called into question. In this intriguing and provocative collection of talks, Robert Mann addresses many of the issues which confront Buddhism as it adapts to modern western culture. Rebirth and traditional cosmology, the role of ethics in 20th-century consumer society, the dangers inherent in confusing therapy with spirituality - these are just some of the topics included in this controversial book.

*Covers in an admirably clear manner the fundamentals of the Buddhadharma... a book to be recommended - **Amadeo Solé-Leris, Journal of Buddhist Ethics***

*A pleasure to read - lucid, unambiguous and expressive - **Buddhism Now***

MODERN BUDDHISM

Alan and Jacqui James

*'The Buddha's Teaching is as relevant today as it ever has
been. It describes the facts of human life which are observable
by anyone who cares to take the trouble to investigate.'*

Presenting timeless truths in a twentieth-century context,
Modern Buddhism provides answers to questions that have
always haunted mankind.

Dying and death: A wasted and terrifying experience – or an
opportunity for spiritual growth? A meditation teacher
describes the way she helped her mother approach the doors
of death.

Family relationships: Why do some families live in harmony
whilst other are constantly at war? What is the purpose of
the family unit?

Heterosexuality/homosexuality/celibacy: What sexual habits
are most conducive to progress along the path?

Alan and Jacqui James belong to the tradition of teachers
who present the essence of Buddhism in a way which is
totally in tune with the needs of their own time and culture.

*In a confused and dark world, the book is like a ray of light
showing the path to sanity and peace –*

Buddhism Today, Brisbane

LIFE AS A SIAMESE MONK

Richard Randall

May 1954, Bangkok – 10,000 people converge on the outlying temple of Wat Paknam to witness an historic ceremony. Forty-seven year old journalist-photographer Richard Randall is taking the saffron robe to ordain as a Buddhist monk. Known henceforth as Kapilavaddho Bhikkhu, he is the first Englishman to enter the monkhood in Thailand.

The ordination itself forms part of an initiation into the sixteen-body practice, one of the little-known systems of Buddhist meditation. This practice Kapilavaddho is to perfect as he travels into increasingly refined levels of mind. He journeys through the psychic realms and back into his own past lives. He comes to understand that the heart of the Buddha's Teaching can be found only in this life, here and now.

Now published for the first time, this is the story of the man who later did so much to introduce Buddhist meditation to the West. It is the autobiography of a true pioneer who more than lived up to his name, Kapilavaddho – He who spreads and increases the Teaching.

*An exceptionally fine Dhamma-read – **Buddhism Now***

*An inspiring story of Buddhist devotion – **Light of Peace, Bangkok***

BUDDHIST CHARACTER ANALYSIS

Robert Mann & Rose Youd

Food, sleep, relationships, sex: do you go for quality, quantity or moderation? Or would you prefer to live without them?

Buddhist Character Analysis is a practical guide to the infinite complexities of human behaviour.

You're offered your own TV show. Do you think, 'What took them so long?' Or would you rather die?

Based exclusively on observable facts, *Buddhist Character Analysis* identifies our fundamental motives and assumptions.

Does your heart sink at the prospect of a quiet weekend? Or do you believe that the world could be a wonderful place if it wasn't for all those people?

Skilful use of *Buddhist Character Analysis* leads to a greater understanding of human nature and increasing happiness in daily life.

How do you see the enlightened person? An aloof Himalayan hermit, master of self-control? Or a charismatic leader using his powers to create a better world?

Combined with a spiritual training, *Buddhist Character Analysis* deepens insight into the true nature of reality.

A thoroughly readable introduction to the subject -
Holistic London Guide

These books are available by mail-order:

The Unfolding of Wisdom
  softback   £8.95
  hardback   £10.95
Modern Buddhism   £7.95
Buddhism in a Foreign Land   £8.50
Buddhist Character Analysis   £6.95
Life as a Siamese Monk   £8.95

(Prices include postage and packing)

Please send to:

Aukana Trust
9 Masons Lane
Bradford on Avon BA15 1QN